DEM⬤S

Demos is an independent think tank committed to radical thinking on the long-term problems facing the UK and other advanced industrial societies.

It aims to develop ideas – both theoretical and practical – to help shape the politics of the twenty first century, and to improve the breadth and quality of political debate.

Demos publishes books and a quarterly journal and undertakes substantial empirical and policy oriented research projects. Demos is a registered charity.

In all its work Demos brings together people from a wide range of backgrounds in business, academia, government, the voluntary sector and the media to share and cross-fertilise ideas and experiences.

For further information and
subscription details please contact:
Demos
9 Bridewell Place
London EC4V 6AP
Telephone: 0171 353 4479
Facsimile: 0171 353 4481
email: mail@demos.co.uk

Other publications available from Demos:

The self-policing society
The common sense of community
The rise of the social entrepreneur
Life after politics: new thinking for the 21st century

To order a publication or
a free catalogue please contact
Demos (details overleaf).

Turning the tide
crime, community and prevention

Jon Bright

DEM☉S

First published in 1997 by
Demos
9 Bridewell Place
London EC4V 6AP
Telephone: 0171 353 4479
Facsimile: 0171 353 4481
email: mail@demos.co.uk
© Demos 1997

Paper No. 27
ISBN 1 898309 33 7
Printed in Great Britain by EG Bond Ltd
Designed by Lindsay Nash
Thanks to Adrian Taylor

Contents

Acknowledgments

This book draws on the work of many academics, policy makers and practitioners, whose contributions I hope are adequately referenced. In particular, I would like to acknowledge the following: my colleagues at Crime Concern, especially Kevin Gill, Oliver Goode, Tony Holden, Sohail Husain, Margaret Mary Kelly, Julia Stafford, Leslie Silverlock, Pamela McAllister and Nigel Whiskin; John Graham and Gloria Laycock of the Home Office; David Farrington of the University of Cambridge; Nick Tilley of Nottingham Trent University; Steve Osborn of the Safe Neighbourhoods Unit; David Utting of the Joseph Rowntree Foundation; and David Hawkins and Richard Catalano of the University of Washington, Seattle.

This book is influenced significantly by visits to the United States in 1990-91, sponsored by the Commonwealth Fund of New York Harkness Fellowships Programme, and in 1996, sponsored by the Joseph Rowntree Foundation. I am very grateful to both organisations for making those invaluable visits possible. It is also informed by contacts with other European countries, notably France and the Netherlands, and with Australia.

I would like to thank the following for commenting on earlier drafts of the book: Tony Butler, Chief Constable of Gloucestershire; Paul Ekblom and John Graham of the Home Office; Kevin Gill and Nigel Whiskin of Crime Concern; Geraldine Petterssen, Associate Consultant with Crime Concern; and Perri 6, Research Director of Demos. Their comments helped me to improve it considerably. They are not of course responsible for its overall style or conclusions.

The book's focus is residential neighbourhoods, their schools and businesses and the prevention of offending and anti-social behaviour by young people. It does not address 'hidden' crimes (such as domestic violence) or 'white collar' crime. These are important topics that require separate and detailed attention. It does not deal in detail with the work of the criminal justice agencies to prevent re-offending although many of the measures it advocates will support their efforts. Its main argument is that the criminal justice system is not very good at preventing crime, clearing up crime, enhancing community safety, deterring offenders or rehabilitating those who are convicted. Criminal justice policy needs to make a decisive shift towards prevention. There is growing evidence that it would be successful, better value for money and popular.

Jon Bright
March 1997

Crime prevention and community safety – a definition

Crime prevention seeks to reduce the risks of criminal events and related misbehaviour by intervening in their causes. It acts at many levels in society, from institutions to the individual, to influence both offenders and immediate crime situations. It may focus on the general population of offenders or targets of crime (primary prevention), those at risk of offending or victimisation (secondary), and those already convicted or attacked (tertiary). At its widest, prevention embraces preventive functions of policing, and sentences and disposals available to the courts such as imprisonment, probation and community service. At the opposite extreme, it links to informal social control and protective behaviour. It also connects with conflict resolution and broader social and economic policy and practice.

Prevention can also act in anticipation, identifying potential causes of crime and assessing risk, in such fields as planning, design and management of products, systems and environments. It can involve appraising the likely impact on crime of social and economic policies directed towards other ends.

Community safety is an aspect of the quality of life, providing an environment in which people can pursue their social and economic lives free from crime and related misbehaviour, and from the suffering, costs, restrictions and fear it engenders. Community safety is facilitated by crime prevention of all kinds, whether situational or offender orientated; by action specifically against fear; and by wider action which incidentally serves these purposes.

Paul Ekblom
1996

Summary

Recorded crime has risen tenfold since the 1950s. Between 1981 and 1993, it rose by a massive 111 per cent. At a local level, crime is often the number one issue that the public want tackled.

Traditionally we have expected the criminal justice system to deal with crime. Yet Home Office figures show that for every 100 crimes committed, only three result in a caution or conviction. The problem is that the criminal justice system processes crime *after* the event. It cannot manage the current volume of everyday crime and disorder problems encountered by the public in their town centres, neighbour-hoods, schools and on public transport.

Over the past ten years, government departments have begun to support crime prevention programmes. Local crime prevention and community safety partnerships have been developed in many areas, and they have achieved important successes. But the scale of activity to prevent crime remains very small compared to the size of the problem. Less than half of 1 per cent of the criminal justice budget is spent on prevention.

This book advocates a much more serious strategy of prevention, one which creates a *culture of prevention* within both national and local governance. We need a strategy which will set objectives, coordinate the work of government departments, establish a structure for deliv-ering local community safety services and ensure that preventing crime becomes a greater priority for the criminal justice agencies – as the Audit Commission recommended in its recent reports on policing and the juvenile justice system.

A national crime prevention strategy must build on the themes of early childhood prevention, opportunities for young people and safer neighbourhoods. Such a strategy should aim to reduce the risk factors which lead to criminality, such as family conflict, alienation and lack of training or employment opportunities while strengthening 'protective' factors which divert would-be offenders from crime. These include improving parenting, school enrichment, outreach youth work and mentoring, and training and employment programmes. Such measures can strengthen young people's attachment to their family, school and community, which in turn makes them less inclined to behave anti-socially and offend. At the same time, opportunities to commit crime must also be reduced through improving security and design of housing, intensifying the management of social housing, developing problem solving styles of policing.and increasing community involvement. Locally, strategies need to bring together all the relevant agencies, with much more rigorous planning than there has been in the past.

Successful programmes in Britain, the United States and the Netherlands show that preventive measures can work. A pre-school programme in the United States shows convincingly that pre-school participation can increase the proportion of young people who at age nineteen are literate, employed and enrolled in post-secondary education. A summer youth project in the UK, which included a programme of recreational activities for youths in combination with local housing security improvements, benefited from a 29 per cent reduction in crime compared with the same months of the previous year. In the Netherlands, a cross-ministry programme is successfully tackling high unemployment, immigration and the social and cultural divisions which result, including crime and fear of crime.

Here in Britain there are three challenges for a new government. The first is to steer the public and political debate on crime away from an obsession with sentencing (what to do with *offenders*) towards prevention (how to reduce *offending*). The second is to find ways of redirecting resources from reacting to crime to preventing it. The third is to ensure we invest in prevention in high crime areas before problems become too big to prevent.

If we can rise to the challenge we can not only improve people's quality of life and reduce fear, but also save huge sums of money that are now spent coping with the effects of crime.

Introduction

In an age of information overload, crime statistics rarely receive the attention necessary to make sense of them. This book begins with ten items of statistical information which will be familiar to those involved in the criminal justice system but hardly known at all to anyone else.

- The ratio of recorded crimes has risen from around one per 100 people in the 1950s to five per 100 in the 1970s to ten per 100 in 1994. Crime recorded by the police represents about only one third of all the crime that takes place.[1]
- Between 1981 and 1993, recorded crime rose by 111 per cent. The rise in crime measured by the *British crime survey* was rather less steep at 77 per cent.[2]
- In 1993-94, £9.42 billion was spent on the criminal justice agencies. Only £240 million (0.37 per cent) is spent by government directly on prevention.[3]
- For every 100 crimes that are committed, 47 are reported to the police, 27 are recorded by them and five are cleared up. Only three out of 100 result in a caution or a conviction.[4]
- One in every three men receives a conviction for a standard list offence by age 40.[5] Crime is mainly (although by no means exclusively) a problem caused by males.
- Two thirds of offenders aged under 21 sentenced to probation, community service or prison between 1987 and 1990 were reconvicted within two years.[6]

- Fifty five per cent of young men and 31 per cent of young women admit to committing a crime at some time during their lives although most commit only one or two offences. About 3 per cent of offenders are responsible for over one quarter of all offences.[7]
- Young men are not growing out of crime as they reach their late teens and early twenties. In fact, property offending may now be increasing with age up to the mid twenties.[8]
- Crime costs central and local government, the private sector and individuals many billions of pounds. Coopers & Lybrand suggest £16.7 billion, a figure which includes the cost of the criminal justice system. The precise figure for particular crimes is difficult to quantify but estimates have been made for burglary (£1 billion), car crime (£750 million), arson (£500 million) and crime against business (£5 billion).[9]
- The public overwhelmingly and consistently cite crime as one of their three main concerns.[10]

In this book, I argue for a crime management policy that is grounded in prevention. Section one reviews existing policy and notes the imbalance in public expenditure between reacting to crime and preventing it. It discusses one of the main obstacles to advancing the case for prevention, namely the limited public confidence in the ability of the criminal justice system to deal effectively and fairly with young offenders, protect the public from dangerous offenders and (with other agencies) make public spaces safer. It argues that while these issues dominate the debate about crime, it will be difficult to promote more serious consideration about prevention.

Section two aims to demolish some of the most common myths about crime and its prevention. The first is that 'nothing works' because crime rates are determined by social forces beyond the reach of policy intervention. The second is that crime prevention is a matter for the criminal justice system. The third is that crime prevention is mainly a matter for communities. The fourth is that there is a single solution. Demolishing these myths paves the way for a discussion about what might work.

Section three presents a framework for prevention which has three themes:

- early childhood prevention
- opportunities for young people
- safer neighbourhoods.

It considers why we need to invest in both crime and criminality prevention and introduces the concepts of risk and protective factors. It suggests that the purpose of prevention is to reduce the risk factors associated with criminality and other 'problem behaviours', such as drug misuse, to strengthen the factors which protect against them and to reduce opportunities for crime. It notes that many preventive measures have multiple benefits of which the prevention of crime and criminality is but one. It discusses each theme in turn, reviewing the approaches for which there is evidence of success. It argues that priority should be given to implementing a customised package of preventive measures in high crime neighbourhoods, drawing, where possible, on all three themes.

Section four suggests how a local prevention strategy might be developed. It considers how to make multi-agency partnerships more effective, reviews the limitations of current crime prevention work and argues that a systematic, problem solving approach is more likely to make a sustained impact. It emphasises that priorities should be agreed, following a proper analysis of crime, risk factors and local resources. It pays particular attention to the difficulties of implementing multi-agency programmes. In doing so, it stresses the value of effective leadership and management. It notes that new resources are needed but often much better preventive use can be made of existing services. It ends by suggesting the preconditions for a durable community safety strategy.

Section five explores the role of central government. This involves providing political leadership, framing a national strategy, avoiding legislation that unintentionally increases crime and ensuring that prevention informs 'whole of government' policy. An important task for government is to place a duty on local authorities and police authorities to prepare annual, costed crime prevention and community safety plans. It argues that we have to think beyond individual crime prevention initiatives. We need to consider how prevention can be 'mainstreamed' and become a core function of central and local governance. It continues with a discussion of costs and benefits and argues that prevention can be a cost effective means of preventing many types of crime. It describes a preventive strategy involving contracts between central and local government that has been developed in the Netherlands.

The book concludes that exhortations against anti-social behaviour, drug misuse and crime are, on their own, unlikely to make a difference. Action is needed to promote a greater sense of individual responsibility and attachment to society among those most likely to offend. It recommends that 'tried and tested' preventive practice should be implemented on a much greater scale. We know a great deal about it; there would be considerable public support for it; it is good policy; and it is cost effective. The time is ripe for a radical shift in the way we think about crime. We spend a very large amount reacting to crime after it has occurred. We need to do much more to prevent it from happening in the first place.

1. Crime, prevention and protection

Crime and prevention

Crime rates (recorded and self-reported) have risen steadily since the early 1960s and surveys reveal consistently that crime is one of the most pressing problems, particularly for the residents of low income urban communities. Crime rates are much higher in such areas and some people are repeatedly victimised. The impact of crime on these victims is often compounded by their poverty and inability to protect themselves, and by the failure of the statutory agencies to provide adequate protection and to deal with the perpetrators. In addition, such areas are invariably characterised by high levels of anti-social behaviour and disorder which heighten fear of crime.[11]

However, crime is not only a problem for the poor. Its effects leak into neighbouring areas. The middle classes living in inner urban neighbourhoods are often heavily victimised.[12] Small businesses in many areas experience very high levels of crime.[13] Town and city centres can be blighted and crime has been increasing in rural areas.[14] Random violence, although rare, can affect anyone anywhere. Domestic violence does not respect class divisions.[15] Violence against children in schools in the form of bullying can be commonplace and is as much a problem for middle class as for working class children.[16] Fear of crime is pervasive, even in areas where there is little justification for it.[17]

Over the past ten years, a great deal has been done to address these problems. Among many initiatives, the Home Office has promoted an approach to crime prevention based on partnerships between the police, local authorities, the private sector and other agencies, has set up Safer Cities projects in 40 towns and cities and has made funds available for installing closed circuit television. The Department of the Environment has funded security and design improvements to housing estates and the Department for Education and Employment has sponsored youth crime prevention programmes. Drug Action Teams have been set up to help tackle drug-related crime. Local authorities and the police, together with the private and voluntary sectors, have developed many local initiatives.

Yet much of this action has been on a small scale. Crime prevention remains a peripheral function for most agencies (including the police) and a core function for none. Most of the £9.4 billion annual expenditure on the criminal justice system is spent reacting to crime rather than preventing it. Although there have been many developments over the past ten years, much crime prevention is unfocused and amateurish, both in its conception and delivery.

With one or two notable exceptions, there have been few attempts to apply the knowledge drawn from special projects to mainstream practice. The substantial amount of energy and commitment devoted to prevention over the past ten years does not amount to a national strategy. Indeed, it sometimes seems that the whole is rather less than the sum of its parts. What is needed is a more coherent attempt to agree priorities, mobilise resources and apply what we know works.

This is still some way off. In a speech in June 1995, David Smith, Professor of Criminology at the University of Cambridge, described the decade 1985 to 1995 as the 'early modern period' of crime prevention characterised by: experimentation; few resources; little evaluation; a 'shotgun' approach to problem solving; a reliance on voluntary partnerships; and no training or professional standards. He suggested there were inherent problems with the current arrangements. At a national level, government has found it difficult to articulate a national strategy and coordinate the work of its own departments. At a local level, he argues, there is a confusing range of active groups and the respective roles of these, the police and local authorities are unclear. Few areas have developed durable strategies, local projects do not learn from one another and there is no accumulation of experience and knowledge.[18]

David Smith's analysis helps us understand why crime prevention policy is so underdeveloped. First, it is a relatively new policy area which requires a coordinated response from a number of government departments. This is never easy to achieve. Second, there is no agreement about how to address aspects of the problem, for example, the prevention of criminality. Hence there is no vision of what can be achieved. Third, there is often resistance to change from key agencies. This underdevelopment of policy is reflected in political and public debate about crime which remains persistently fixated on sentencing (what to do about offenders) rather than prevention (how to prevent people becoming offenders).

A long-term goal of any government should be to reduce the number of people who offend. This can be done by creating a culture of prevention so that prevention becomes integral to national and local governance. For this to be achieved, it must be shown to be a cost effective means of dealing with crime and related problems. Strategic leadership is required from central government. The subject must become a statutory responsibility for local government and police authorities. Incentives are needed to encourage public and private institutions to prioritise prevention. Most importantly, it must secure the confidence of the public and their political representatives. This is most likely to happen if the public has confidence in the criminal justice system as a whole and feels that reasonable steps are being taken to protect them from the crimes they fear most.

Prevention and protection

At present the public does not have this confidence. Many people feel that the criminal justice system is ineffective.[19] In particular, they think that youth crime and anti-social behaviour are not being tackled firmly, there is not enough being done to protect them from dangerous offenders and public spaces are less safe than they should be. Until the public feels that these primary concerns have been addressed satisfactorily, it will be more difficult to advance the case for prevention. Let us examine each of them in turn.

The first concern is the perceived lack of a convincing policy for young offenders, at least in England and Wales. During the 1970s and 1980s, there was widespread support by all political parties and professionals for limiting the use of imprisonment, using non-custodial penalties and, wherever possible, diverting young people from the criminal justice system altogether. Since 1993, this consensus has broken down. Those advocating a 'tougher' approach argue that these 'liberal' policies have not stemmed the rise in crime nor diverted young people from offending or re-offending. They claim greater use of custody is needed to deal more punitively with offenders (both young and adult) and reassure the public.

Those defending the consensus deny that 'prison works'. Re-offending rates after release are high. Prison is an inappropriate and expensive way of dealing with the majority of offenders who do not pose a threat to the public. They argue that it is particularly harmful for juveniles and young adults on whom it may confirm a criminal identity and thereby increase the likelihood that they will re-offend. As a result of 'tougher' policies, they point out, the prison population is now at its highest level ever. They fear the development of an American-style 'incarceration' response to crime in the UK.

This highly controversial shift in policy did not occurred solely because policy making in the Home Office was taken over by those with hardline attitudes to offenders. The consensus which advocated minimal use of custody and promoted community-based sentences was always vulnerable because some of its foundations were weak. Two criticisms in particular have been levelled against it. First, it appears to emphasise the welfare of offenders at the expense of the protection of the public. Second, it did not lead to significant and convincing action to reduce youth crime.

Crime and fear of crime rose throughout the 1980s and early 1990s to become one of the public's top three concerns. This cannot be explained wholly by media-induced 'moral panics', as some have tried to do. Crime in many urban areas is high and fear is justified. The public, particularly people living in such areas, do not always feel reassured by community penalties and other measures to keep young offenders out of the criminal justice system. They want action that will prevent crime and make them feel safer.

The gap between the official response to young offenders and the public experience of crime was most apparent when, in 1994, official crime figures showed that there had been a significant reduction in juvenile crime during the previous decade.[20] This seemed to suggest that diverting young offenders from the criminal justice system was also reducing their offending. Yet, as David Farrington, Professor of Psychological Criminology at the University of Cambridge, points out, this 'official' reduction in juvenile crime was largely illusory. It is explained by an increase in non-recorded informal warnings by the police, a reduction in police detection rates for property crimes, the downgrading of certain crimes (such as theft from motor vehicles) from indictable to summary offences, the effect of the Police and Criminal Evidence Act and the introduction of the Crown Prosecution Service in 1986.[21]

It seemed highly unlikely in any case that juvenile crime was decreasing during a period when recorded crime had increased by 50 per cent. Given the scale of this increase, it is probable that offending by juveniles increased between 1984 and 1994. We know, for example, that during this ten year period, there was a 15 per cent increase in the number of eighteen to twenty year olds who were cautioned or convicted. The coalition of interests advocating diversion as the main response to non-violent youth crime did so for the best of reasons. However, diverting young offenders *from* the criminal justice system is not a sufficient response to offending if they are not at the same time diverted *to* something which is going to challenge their offending behaviour. In the 1980s and early 1990s, fewer juvenile offenders were cautioned or convicted at a time when youth crime was increasing. As a result public confidence in the system was undermined.

It is increasingly accepted that major reform of the system for dealing with young offenders is needed.[22] Let us consider some specific shortcomings. At present, offenders wait, on average, four to five months before attending court. Delays make it make it more difficult for the court process to influence behaviour.[23] There are considerable geographic variations in the provision of bail hostels and secure accommodation which means that many persistent offenders carry on offending; it has been estimated that between one quarter and one third of juveniles offend while on bail.[24] Even when a case is decided by the youth court, the outcome is often unsatisfactory.

Community sentences are often inadequate. Many do not receive adequate supervision and it occurs too late in their offending career to make a difference. Of a sample of convicted ten to seventeen year olds, half were conditionally discharged without supervision, one fifth were ordered to attend attendance centres and only one fifth were placed on a programme aimed at changing their behaviour.[25] Of these, many will see a social worker for one hour a week or even less. There are no national figures on re-offending after community supervision but four fifths of a sample of 275 seventeen year olds given community sentences in 1991 were reconvicted within two years.[26] The Association of Directors of Social Services and the National Association of Care and Resettlement of Offenders (NACRO) have commented that programmes are uneven and inadequate in number and variety, and that there are too many gaps in provision.[27]

The youth justice system needs to deal with offenders promptly and strike a more convincing balance between the welfare of the offender and the protection of the community. Secure accommodation will be required to control the most persistent offenders. For the majority, custodial sentences should be avoided where possible but community sentences should be rigorous and intensive. This may involve the use of personalised 'action plans' involving education, training and mentoring options and, if appropriate, more supervision over an extended period of time.[28] Cautioning should continue to be used for the least serious offenders but, where appropriate, linked to action designed to change their behaviour. Generally, the prime focus for most young offenders must be on prevention.

A second reason for public disenchantment with the criminal justice system is the widespread perception that it does not protect them from dangerous offenders. Although small in number, these are the people the public fear most.[29] There is a perception that many men who persistently assault women and children are being released after serving short or modest sentences or are given early parole, even when it is known that there is a high risk of their re-offending.

There has been a number of cases where predatory paedophiles with a history of addictive offending involving escalating violence towards children have been freed, even though it is in the nature of their condition that they will offend again. It has been estimated that there are 5,000 convicted paedophiles living in the community unsupervised or under minimal supervision.[30] The true number will be much higher because it is difficult to catch such offenders, bring cases to court and secure convictions. During 1996, this topic started to receive the attention its seriousness demands and proposals to monitor paedophiles and supervise them more effectively were included in the 1996 Crime (Sentences) Bill.

There have also been well-publicised murders committed by psychiatric patients released into the community. The closure of hospitals without adequate funding of community mental health services has prompted the Royal College of Psychiatrists to admit that their members often have no alternative but to release long-term, severely mentally ill patients into the community without support or supervision in order to free up beds. Inevitably, some of these patients constitute a danger to the public.[31]

It is often argued that the statistical risk of violent crime is very low and there is no evidence that the problem is worsening. Those who fear the most (such as the elderly) are least at risk and fear of violent crime is out of all proportion to its incidence. It is also true that most violent crime against women and children occurs in the home. It is therefore illogical for women to be unduly fearful of violence from strangers or for parents to cocoon their children.

Such arguments do not reassure people because a high proportion of the adult population knows someone who has experienced a serious offence and because each year there are a horrific attacks and murders committed by people who have recently been released from prison or hospital. As a result, the public loses confidence in the ability of the system to assess risk properly, detain dangerous people and thereby protect them. Because these crimes, although statistically rare, are random, unpredictable and so appalling, the public – especially women and children – feel they have to be alert at all times.

The perception that the state is not doing as much as it could to protect the public from sexual and violent offenders increases fear of crime, stokes up the 'tough on crime' rhetoric and makes it more difficult to promote prevention and the use of non-custodial sentences for those non-violent offenders who are a danger to no one. Action is needed to bring more sex offenders to court. Convicted violent offenders likely to pose a continuing threat to the community if released should be retained in custody or secure care. Sexual and violent offenders who are released into the community should be more intensively supervised. Where there is real doubt, as there often is, about the risk to the public involved in releasing violent patients or offenders, the public should more often be given the benefit of that doubt.

The third issue which concerns the public is the observation that not enough is done to protect people in public spaces – in town and city centres, on public transport, in parks, around schools and on the street. Again, it is not enough simply to point out that real risks of victimisation may be low. These places often feel uncomfortable because they are poorly maintained, disorderly, underused or unsupervised. Any stranger could behave unpredictably and possibly criminally and, if they did, there would be no one to deal with it. People invariably express this disquiet as fear of crime. They avoid these areas when they can, thereby contributing to the depopulation which in turn generates more fear.

It is unrealistic to think that all public areas could be rendered safe all the time. However, all towns and cities have their 'symbolic locations'. These are the central squares or shopping centres, centres of entertainment, business areas, main parks and the pedestrian routes linking them with car parks and public transport facilities. In residential neighbourhoods, they are the pedestrian routes between housing, shopping areas, schools and main public transport routes. These can and should be made safer. There are sufficient examples of where this has been done well to justify widespread replication.[32]

Perceptions of fear in public spaces become all the more important when we consider current trends in crime and fear of crime. Criminologists Tony Bottoms and Paul Wiles have observed that 'late modern society' is characterised by community fragmentation, increased personal insecurity, social isolation and a decline in community cohesion and the stability of the family.

They note how our cities are in danger of dividing into two types of areas. On the one hand, there are the shopping malls, office complexes and up-market estates which are privately owned, safe, well policed and able to exclude those who are considered undesirable. On the other, there are social housing estates and public spaces which have minimum levels of policing and low levels of social control, which are termed the 'badlands'.[33]

Insecurity and public concern about crime will probably increase if no effective and sustained action is taken. Some of the issues raised in this chapter pose difficult problems for public policy. For others, there are obvious solutions that could and should be implemented promptly. Reforming the youth justice system, responding to public concern about sexual and violent offenders and doing more to improve safety in public areas may create a more favourable climate in which the obvious next step is more investment in the prevention of crime and criminality. Before considering the type of preventive measures that might be promoted, it is necessary to demolish some myths about crime and its prevention.

2. Demolishing myths

The previous chapter examined some public concerns about crime and showed that the perceived failure to respond to these explains why the debate about crime always seems to concentrate on what to do *after* a crime has been committed rather than how to prevent crime and criminality in the first place. In order to steer the debate towards more 'upstream' prevention, it is also important to consider – and refute – some of the dominant views about the prevention of crime that have acquired the status of 'folklore' or myths.

Myth one: nothing much can be done

There are some – mainly academics – who argue that crime rises and falls as a result of 'deep' social and economic forces that are not susceptible to policy intervention. Crime prevention projects have little effect. Even if they do, the crimes they prevent will probably be displaced and any improvements that are achieved will not be sustained. There is, therefore, not much to be done other than encourage individuals to take precautionary action, try to avoid legislation which inadvertently increases crime and leave the criminal justice agencies to cope.

It is true that levels of crime are affected by social and economic forces. For example, we know that crime is related to levels of consumption, to the Gross Domestic Product, to unemployment and to economic growth. One economist has argued that half the reduction in property crime between 1993 and 1995 can be explained by short-term improvements in the economy.[34] We also know that crime is affected by the number of young males in the population, the extent to which people feel they have a stake in society and so on.

This argument suggests that there is probably a hypothetical threshold below which crime is unlikely to fall, unless investment in prevention were to rise to quite unrealistic levels, because of the particular economic, cultural and demographic characteristics of this country. We do not know what this threshold is and it will fluctuate with changes in these characteristics. The volume of crime between this threshold and the actual level at any one time is therefore theoretically preventable. Since crime prevention is a relatively new area of social policy and has received only modest levels of funding, it is unlikely that we are close to this threshold.

Government is, therefore, not powerless to act. Even if it is constrained by the forces of a globalised economy, it still has some scope to mitigate the impact of problems such as youth unemployment, school failure and family dysfunction. Quality training and employment programmes for at risk young people can reduce their offending significantly. Similarly, policies to help schools reduce school failure, truancy and exclusion can also impact on criminality. Policies which support families, improve parenting and reduce family stress and breakdown also reduce child abuse and the cycle of violence with which it is associated. There is a good deal of research (to be discussed later) which shows that policy interventions can be effective in reducing crime and offending.

A variant of the 'nothing can be done' myth is that nothing works because prevention is not robust enough to make an impact on something as 'hard' as crime. This view was originally expressed by Robert Martinson in the early 1970s, although by 1978 he had renounced his earlier work.[35] Nevertheless, it is probable that many policy makers privately hold this view.

That scepticism is understandable. Much prevention is not very convincing. It does need to become more rigorous and demonstrably successful. This can be achieved by ensuring that it is properly targeted and designed to bring about real reductions in crime or offending. When this approach is followed, the results can be impressive. The methodology of prevention is discussed fully in chapter four.

There is one school of thought which argues that 'not much can be done' because the cost to the 'culture of contentment' middle classes who live in low crime areas of the kinds of intervention needed to impact on crime are unacceptably great and the benefits to them not readily apparent. There are also some merits, it is argued, in leaving some areas of the country to crime and criminals. Protagonists of this view would suggest that there is no public and political support for significant expansion in preventive activity.

Let us consider the validity of this view. Crime rates in all areas rose between 1984 and 1993 and started to rise again in 1996. Crime rates in rural areas rose faster than in the cities. The middle classes cannot distance themselves from these problems unless they want to confine themselves to secure compounds. In any case, many live in areas with relatively high crime rates. They use public transport, visit town and city centres, and use schools and NHS facilities, all of which are troubled by crime problems. Those from low crime areas may also be concerned about their children who may not live in comfortable, safe neighbourhoods.

Furthermore, building more prisons to house the increasing number of offenders that may result from a failure to invest more in prevention is a very expensive option. If chosen, it will almost certainly be at the expense of spending less on education, health and public transport. Better value for money could be secured by redirecting some of this towards prevention.

Reduced crime and enhanced safety would bring direct benefits in terms of reduced fear of crime and the consequent greater freedom to enjoy all that a modern urban culture has to offer. There is also a powerful moral argument: many of the 'content' middle classes still believe in a civic society and would not want to see greater social divisions or the further segregation of our towns and cities. There is already considerable public alarm over the apparent decline in civic responsibility and social cohesion. When asked, the public support measures to prevent crime, especially that committed by young people.[36] The costs of not investing in prevention may be felt in an escalating prison population with all the associated expenditure, the drift into crime of an increasing number of poor young men and cities which few will want to live in or visit.

There are also those (such as some newspaper columnists) who argue that nothing should be done if it involves unwarranted interference by the state in the private domain, as some preventive measures undoubtedly do. For example, measures to reduce criminality may involve advising parents on parenting styles and encouraging them to become more involved in their children's education. This may be seen as intrusive but participation is invariably voluntary and people can, if they choose, reject it. Moreover, the consequences of poor parenting and school failure can lead to much more involuntary intrusion from the state. Modest, voluntary and sensitively delivered prevention aimed at parents and their children can bring great benefits and is often valued highly.

Having and raising children is not a totally private act. As one commentator has observed, it is 'an act that has significant consequences for the whole community.'[37] The state has a right to promote prevention among those most at risk of crime and criminality on the grounds that the financial and social costs of crime to the state, the private sector and the individual are greater than the costs of prevention. The alternative – relying on sentencing policy and the criminal justice system to control crime – has not been noticeably effective.

Finally, some human biologists argue that nothing can be done because a high proportion of all crime is caused by chemical imbalances in the brain and that pharmaco-therapy is needed at an early age to remedy these imbalances. Some geneticists argue that there are genes that predispose people to certain types of crime which will be triggered in certain types of environment.

While biology and genetics may explain the motivation of some individual offenders, such determinism conflicts with everything we know about human development. Most experts believe that human behaviour results from a complex interaction between nature and nurture and that it cannot be crudely reduced to biology in this way.

The argument that nothing can be done has been overstated. While it may be difficult to make a sustained and measurable impact on aggregate crime rates, there is considerable scope for reducing crime at a local level.

Myth two: the criminal justice system prevents crime

The criminal justice agencies (the police, courts, probation and prison services) obviously have a major role to play in responding to crime. Most lay people and many politicians think that they are also the principal prevention agencies and believe that if the police detect crime, the courts sentence offenders and the prisons and probation service discharge those sentences, crime will be prevented.

Similarly, many hold the view that the decision to offend is a purely rational choice based on a calculation of the costs and risks involved. Criminal justice policy therefore needs to ratchet up sentences so that the costs and risks to the would-be offender outweigh the potential benefits of offending and the offender is thereby deterred.

The evidence for the effectiveness of this approach is not strong. The formal processes of the criminal justice system – apprehending, prosecuting, sentencing, punishing and rehabilitating offenders – have only a limited effect in controlling crime.[38] There is little evidence that people are deterred from offending by the threat of tough sentences or that detection and conviction deters them from future offending (although the recent police policy of targeting persistent offenders does have a short-term impact on local crime rates and often provides a much-needed respite for the community).[39] Increases in police manpower do not necessarily lead to reduced crime.[40] Rates of recidivism following release from prison remain high and therapeutic treatment is relatively ineffective.[41]

We have already noted how only a small amount crime is cleared up by the system. The criminal justice agencies deal effectively with most serious, violent crime but this constitutes a small proportion of all the crime that takes place. The resources of the criminal justice system are therefore devoted to responding to between 5 and 10 per cent of all crime committed. Accordingly, most recent discussion about crime prevention has focused on the role of agencies outside the criminal justice system.

This view is confirmed by an audit of the criminal justice system in Milton Keynes undertaken by researchers from the University of Sheffield at the invitation of the local police commander. The audit found that only one fifth of crimes were detected and only one in ten resulted in a caution or conviction. This means that offenders were not held to account for nearly nine out of ten crimes committed. This is, admittedly, a little better than the national average but hardly represents good value for money. Moreover, only 1 per cent of the budget of the criminal justice agencies is spent on crime prevention. The Sheffield researchers concluded that a more effective use of resources would be to place much more emphasis on prevention.[42]

The United States provides us with a case study of what happens when a society tries to control crime through the criminal justice system. The increase in the use of imprisonment between 1970 and 1990 was paralleled with an equally steep rise in the rate of reported crime over the same period.[43] The huge increase in imprisonment has probably kept the crime rate slightly lower than it would have been but its impact has been small relative to the investment.[44] The United States now imprisons four times as many people per capita as the UK. A 1990 study found that the prison population is rising by a massive 13 per cent each year. Maintaining that rate of growth costs $100 million a week just for constructing new facilities. Even advocates of tough law and order policies accept that the country cannot afford to finance an unlimited prison building boom and that alternatives must be found.[45]

Moreover, the criminal justice agencies in many jurisdictions are absolutely overwhelmed by the amount of crime they are required to process. In one major American city, plea bargaining for serious felonies and a lack of prison space means that serious offenders are receiving unduly short sentences. Many misdemeanours are simply ignored. Three quarters of the adults who are on probation are not supervised by probation officers. One half of the adults on probation who are supposed to be periodically tested for illegal drugs are not tested. Offenders on probation who commit robbery or burglary are not charged with those crimes but only with violating the terms of their probation in order to ease jail overcrowding and to reduce court caseloads.

If more than 5 per cent of cases go to trial, judicial gridlock sets in. The same people are being repeatedly processed through the system. Any deterrent effect that may have been created by the certainty of swift and sure punishment has been eroded by a system which can no longer cope. Convicted offenders are not receiving appropriate sentences, or being rehabilitated, community safety is being compromised and crime is certainly not being prevented. These problems are probably mirrored to a greater or lesser extent in most of the country's largest cities.[46]

In spite of its heavy use of imprisonment, the United States continues to have by far the highest rate of crime and violence of all developed countries even though crime rates fell between 1991 and 1995. As the federal judge who was chairman of the 1986 President's Commission on Organised Crime remarked: 'Law enforcement has been tested to the utmost, but let's face it, it just hasn't worked.'[47]

Policing and its limits
This is not to argue that the police and, to a lesser extent, the other criminal justice agencies, have no part to play in crime prevention. The police hold the information about crime and offenders and are the only agency trained, equipped and authorised to confront most crime problems. Community crime prevention initiatives are unlikely to work unless there is an appropriate police input and in many cases this may be a precondition for community mobilisation and activity by other agencies. A number of community policing programmes have been demonstrably successful. There is certainly scope for significantly increasing the police contribution to prevention through enhancing their role in delivering local crime prevention strategies.

However, there is a tendency to overstate their role. Most of the work of the police is still reactive rather than preventive. It is not their job to intervene in many of the circumstances which lead to crime being committed. They do not make decisions about the deployment and management of staff in housing estates, schools, youth clubs and shopping centres (although they may be invited to advise). They are not responsible for the enforcement of tenancy regulations, the maintenance of street lighting, the provision of public transport or the design of new commercial and residential developments (all of which impact on crime and disorder). As David Smith observed in 1983:

> The police are not for the main part the prime movers, the initiators of the processes that control deviant behaviour. On the contrary, they work at the margins where the usual processes of

control have broken down . . . they act as a continuation of . . . more general efforts by the mass of people and institutions to maintain order, control and coherence. In other words, they are a small but extremely important element within a much larger complex of interrelated systems of control.[48]

More recently, the 1996 Audit Commission report *Streetwise: effective police patrol* noted that:

The essential role of other agencies (in crime prevention and community safety) is illustrated by the findings of a central Scotland survey of local communities' needs. Only one demand – a visible police presence to reassure and deter anti-social behaviour – is solely a police responsibility. The others fall squarely within the remit of the local authority and other agencies: education on drug and alcohol abuse, improved street lighting, safer play areas, more leisure facilities, road safety measures and attention to environmental concerns such as dogs fouling pavements and parks.[49]

The Commission's own survey confirmed the importance of community safety work undertaken by agencies other than the police. It also identified another desired contribution to safer neighbourhoods – responsible parenting and 'a more disciplined attitude among children and young adults'.

It is possible that the criminal justice agencies – especially the police – reduce fear of crime and enhance safety by their very presence (providing they are visible), even if they have little effect on crime. Yet repeated surveys draw attention to the high level of public concern about crime, which is partly caused by the low visibility of the police. The Audit Commission found that 50 per cent of police personnel were engaged in specialist headquarters functions and only 5 per cent of the remainder were on patrol in the community at any one time, the equivalent of only one police officer on the streets for every 18,000 citizens.[50]

The police are pulled in three ways. The public want more 'bobbies on the beat'; they want offenders arrested instantly; and they expect the police to deal with organised and serious crime, child abuse and drug trafficking. The police cannot meet all these demands and many police forces have decided to concentrate on intelligence-led policing, targeting persistent offenders and investing in the specialist services needed to detect serious crime.

This refocusing of police resources is at the expense of community reassurance and prevention work, a service for which there is massive public demand. It will therefore need to be provided by others, in addition to the police. This is already happening in some areas. In Northumbria, for example, security patrols recruited from the unemployed have been employed by the local authority (with the support of the police) to patrol town and city centres, an approach that is modelled on the Dutch Civic Guards scheme (see chapter five). Sedgefield Council employ their own security patrol. Swansea Council deploy estate wardens on their housing estates. There is an urgent need for similar, affordable, community warden-type schemes to help restore a sense of civic order to our public spaces and to compensate for the shift of police resources into specialist functions.

The criminal justice agencies have some deterrent effect – there would be more crime without them. They have some preventive effect – not all convicted offenders re-offend. And there is certainly scope for increasing their preventive impact, particularly in connection with reducing re-offending by young people. In addition, the preventive role of the police would be much enhanced if they were to replicate more widely the style of pro-active, problem solving, community policing that has been developed in the United States and trialled in the UK. Crime and disorder have been reduced in many areas as a result of effective police work and the important role of the police in tackling crime and disorder in high crime neighbourhoods is discussed in chapter five.

However, as they currently operate, the main functions of the criminal justice system agencies are to process crime after the event and punish the very small proportion of offenders who are convicted. Their deterrent, preventive and rehabilitative effects are limited and poor value for money. It remains to be seen whether this state of affairs is allowed to continue.

Myth three: communities prevent crime

The third myth is that communities (that is, residents and their organisations) can be the principal force for preventing crime even in those areas where crime problems are most serious. This view has been put forward most strongly by Amitai Etzioni and the communitarian movement. 'Empowering the community' to tackle crime (and drug abuse and other symptoms of urban decay) is frequently invoked as an all-purpose solution by local and national politicians. For some, it seems to have an almost totemic power which blinds them to the reality of community life in many high crime areas.

Can communities prevent crime? They certainly have a vital and important role. Some community organisations have struggled impressively and sometimes successfully against overwhelming problems. However, ten years of research in the UK and United States suggests that their capacity to resolve crime and disorder problems is often overstated.[51]

Anti-crime community activities are least common and least successful in the areas in which they are most needed, namely poor, high crime neighbourhoods. Where they do exist in high crime areas, active participants are more likely to take protective measures and are more prepared to intervene. However, levels of participation are modest at best and there is no 'rub off' effect on non-participants.

Attempting to set up new anti-crime organisations in high crime areas is extremely difficult. Participation is low even when substantial efforts are made to organise people. Rather than uniting communities in outrage or common purpose, crime can undermine the capacity of communities to organise in high crime areas and can divide rather than unite people. Evaluations of community crime prevention initiatives have by and large failed to find clear cut evidence of reduced crime nor have they found evidence of increased levels of interaction, solidarity and intervention, the processes which are supposed to induce informal controls and thereby reduce disorder and crime.

Participation in local crime prevention activities is highest – and success more likely – among people who are moderately concerned about crime. High levels of fear are incapacitating and low levels are demotivating. Community anti-crime organisations are more successful in the moderately cohesive, stable middle and working class, in home-owning neighbourhoods which are sufficiently worried about crime to want to do something about it, where relations with the police are good and where programmes can function without external funding. These are probably the most typical neighbourhoods in the UK. In such areas, local residents are more willing and able to make a greater contribution to community safety than in poorer areas.

The rapid growth of voluntary crime prevention in the form of Neighbourhood Watch (NW) schemes, mainly in such areas as described above, has been impressive. In twelve years, over 120,000 schemes have been set up, covering 5 million homes or 25 per cent of the population. Schemes vary enormously but the main benefits of the best ones include increased contact between neighbours, improvements to home security, reductions in fear of crime and improved relationships with the police.

Research shows clearly in which types of area NW is most successful and confirms the points made above. There is little support for NW in areas where i) the risk of crime is low and there is a strong sense of community and ii) the risk of crime is high and there is little sense of community. There is support for NW where the risk of crime is thought to be high but where there is still satisfaction with the neighbourhood.[52] However, a critical point is reached when increasing crime erodes satisfaction. Reducing crime in such areas may sometimes be a precondition for rebuilding a community. Some NW schemes in high crime, disorganised neighbourhoods where satisfaction is low have made an impact on serious problems, at least in the short term. They are, nevertheless, much more difficult to establish and when they are successful it is usually because of particular circumstances such as a charismatic local leader.

Generally, too much has been expected of both policing and community organisations to resolve crime problems in high crime areas. The police have been expected to compensate for the breakdown of other sources of control and order. Community organisations have been expected to address problems that they have neither the resources nor authority to resolve. We will return to the role of the police and community organisations in chapter five.

Myth four: crime is a single solution problem

There is a common tendency for people to look for single, simple solutions to the crime problem. Among those touted in recent years there have been: more police (by far the most common); tougher sentences and more jails (a close second); crime prevention on the school curriculum (very popular); design changes to social housing estates (the technological quick fix); and so on.

It is generally accepted that there are two ways to prevent crime. The first is to make crime more difficult to commit, more risky and less rewarding by putting in place measures such as better security, increased surveillance and property marking. This is the most commonly understood type of crime prevention and can be applied to most situations in which crime is likely to occur. This approach targets the crime-prone situation rather than the offender. It is sometimes called situational crime prevention.

The second approach aims to prevent criminal behaviour. It addresses the underlying causes of offending and seeks to influence the attitudes and behaviour of those most likely to offend so they are less inclined to do so. This is done by reducing the risk factors long known to be associated with offending (such as poor parenting and school failure) and enhancing protective factors (such as good parenting and school success). This approach targets the potential offender rather than the crime. It is sometimes called social crime prevention or criminality prevention.

Both approaches are essential, particularly in high crime areas. While we know that not every risk factor that is known to contribute to a problem must be removed in order to prevent that problem, it is unlikely that a single preventive measure will be sufficient to impact on crime in most urban areas. This is because high levels of crime and fear of crime reflect multiple problems which need to be addressed by multiple solutions. The needs of communities should be carefully assessed and a customised package of measures adopted. Moreover, research shows that when a package of measures is implemented, the benefits of the whole can be greater than the sum of its parts.[53]

Many practitioners and policy makers often seem to be unaware of this and do not understand that a measure which might have a crime prevention effect may only work in combination with others. As a result, they fail to appreciate the powerful effect that can be achieved by a broad range of projects or interventions.

For example, the prevention of criminality in high crime areas relies on reducing risk factors at different developmental stages (early childhood, primary school years, adolescence) and in different locations (family, school, community, peer group). Improving management or design on an estate with a high child density may not reduce crime or anti-social behaviour unless it is accompanied by play and recreation facilities for children and young people. The benefits from investing in pre-school provision for disadvantaged children will be maximised if they transfer to effective schools and if they live in a well managed neighbourhood. The success of local programmes aimed at preventing young people from drifting into crime will depend partly on whether national economic policies work with or against them.

Summary

This chapter has challenged four of the most common myths about crime and its prevention. The first – that nothing can or should be done – partly reflects an anti-urbanism that has been a feature of British culture for 200 years. It also reflects an underlying pessimism about the ability of our system of governance to resolve or ameliorate social problems.

Myths two, three and four – that crime can be reduced by the criminal justice system, by community action or by other single solutions – have been shown to be oversimplified responses to a complex problem. It is high time these myths were debunked. The consequence of believing them for so long has been the creation of a hugely expensive, inefficient and self-perpetuating criminal justice system, crime rates higher than they need to be, a very high rate of concern about crime and large numbers of young people needlessly drifting into crime. The next chapter proposes an alternative way forward.

3. Towards prevention: a framework for local action

A thematic approach

This book advocates an approach to prevention which aims to reduce the risk factors associated with criminality and other problem behaviours (such as serious drug misuse), to strengthen the factors that protect against them and to reduce opportunities for crime. It argues that these aims can be achieved through local programmes which incorporate the following themes:

- early childhood prevention
- opportunities for young people
- safer neighbourhoods.

This approach can be applied (in an appropriate form) in all neighbourhoods that wish to reduce crime problems now and prevent them occurring in the future. Its most comprehensive form is designed for high crime neighbourhoods with multiple problems. Before discussing each of these themes in turn, the principles that underpin the approach will be considered.

Preventing criminality: risk and protective factors

Research conducted over half a century in a number of Western countries has consistently identified common aspects of family and community life which increase the risk of young people offending.[54] The most important of these are listed in the table opposite.

Although it is not possible to identify any one of these as the 'cause' of delinquency, the likelihood of later criminality increases when

Risk factor	
Family	Parental criminality Poor parental supervision / discipline Low family income / social isolation Family conflict
School	Lack of commitment to school (including truancy) Disruptive behaviour (including bullying) Low achievement School disorganisation
Community	Community disorganisation Availability of drugs Opportunity for crime High child densities
Individual / peer	Alienation / lack of social commitment Early involvement in problem behaviour Peers involved in anti-social behaviour High proportion of unsupervised time spent with peers
Early adulthood	No skills or qualifications Unemployment or low income Homelessness

adverse factors cluster together in a child's background. Those children who experience these factors at their most extreme are at greatest risk of becoming persistent offenders responsible for a disproportionate volume of crime.

The influence which some factors exert over children's behaviour is largely indirect. Low income, poor living conditions and social isolation can be viewed as stress factors on parents which can reduce their ability to provide children with the care, attention and discipline necessary for successful parenting. Other factors, such as poor parental supervision and harsh or inconsistent discipline, have a direct influence on children's behaviour.

Yet as is well known, many young people growing up in apparently unpromising circumstances manage to avoid drifting into persistent anti-social behaviour and crime. Researchers have identified protective factors which seem to protect them from behaving anti-socially and acquiring a criminal record. These include some individual characteristics such as a resilient temperament, intelligence, an outgoing nature and, of course, gender.

However, many of the most significant protective factors (for example, good parenting) are often the opposites of the risk factors (in this instance poor parental supervision) and are introduced when preventive action to reduce risk factors is taken. Protective factors encourage pro-social beliefs and high standards of behaviour. They help 'bond' young people to key social groups such as the family, school and community.

Strengthening protective factors involves three key processes: providing young people with opportunities for involvement in their families, schools and communities; helping them acquire key skills – emotional, cognitive and behavioural – to enable them to take advantage of these opportunities; and recognising and praising them.[55] These processes help them to develop the internal controls which enable them to shift their energies away from offending.[56]

The goal of criminality prevention, therefore, is to reduce risk factors and strengthen protective factors. It is important to intervene early before children are drawn into problem behaviours, to include those at greatest risk and to target multiple problems with multiple interventions. It is often difficult to know if a risk factor (such as disruptive behaviour in school) is a cause of delinquency, a symptom or part of the same underlying anti-social tendency. However, it is when risk factors cluster that the risk of offending is greatest and the need for preventive action most urgent.

Recent Home Office research concluded that the strongest risk factors which relate to young people starting to offend are:

- low parental supervision
- truancy
- conflict within the home
- exclusion from school
- friends or siblings in trouble with the police
- poor school performance.

If a young person experiences four or five of these risk factors, the likelihood of them offending is 80 per cent for males and 60 per cent for females.[57] In order to prevent the onset of offending, it makes sense, therefore, to concentrate on reducing these risk factors in those neighbourhoods where there are relatively high rates of youth crime and other problem behaviours and where young people are exposed to multiple risks.

Targeting neighbourhoods rather than individuals, in the first instance, is the preferred option. Contrary to popular belief, it is actually very difficult to predict which children will become offenders when they are young. One of the most sophisticated studies which tried to do this managed to miss 37 per cent of children who later acquired a criminal record and identified 44 per cent of non-delinquents as potential offenders.[58] In addition, isolating and labelling individual children as potential offenders can be stigmatising and counterproductive. Furthermore, many of the preventive measures discussed in this book operate through strengthening community institutions such as the school and family rather than remedying individual pathologies.

However, if prevention is to work, it will be necessary to ensure that those families, children and young people who are most at risk benefit from neighbourhood-based provision. This is most likely to be achieved by careful targeting based on risk assessment, skilled outreach work and designing projects that people value.

The approach to preventing criminality advocated here draws on American as well as UK experience because there have been many more evaluations of innovative prevention in the United States than elsewhere.[59] This enables us to identify the key elements of successful practice although the process of policy transfer from one country to another must be undertaken with care.

A comprehensive approach: preventing crime and criminality

The programme advocated here does not rely only on measures to reduce risk factors associated with offending. Measures which make crime more difficult, more risky and less rewarding to commit are equally important. Accordingly, the 'Safer neighbourhoods' theme includes situational approaches to crime prevention and community safety such as physical security, environmental design, housing management and policing. As we noted at the end of the last chapter, their focus is on the crime prone situation rather than the offender or potential offender.

The two approaches – crime and criminality prevention – complement and reinforce each other. This is common sense. It will be easier for parents, schools and youth workers to encourage improvements in behaviour if opportunities for crime are reduced and the neighbourhood is adequately managed and policed. Moreover, the measures in the 'Safer neighbourhoods' theme will often have a more immediate impact on crime than some of those listed under 'Early childhood prevention' and 'Opportunities for young people'.

The table opposite lists a range of preventive measures and the risk factors they address.

The thematic structure adopted for this chapter is a useful way of classifying preventive measures. It is not, however, necessary to do everything. The measures listed opposite should be seen as a menu of tried and tested approaches. Priorities should be determined following a careful assessment of crime problems and risk factors in particular neighbourhoods.

For example, a neighbourhood with an above average proportion of eleven to fifteen year olds and high levels of excluded pupils, youth

Theme	Preventive measures	Risk factors addressed
Early childhood prevention	Parenting programmes Family support Pre-school education Family literacy	Poor parental supervision and discipline; alienation and lack of commitment; family conflict; low educational achievement
Opportunities for young people	Organisational change in schools Preventing truancy and exclusion After school activities Intensive youth work Mentoring Skills training Work experience Supported housing	Low achievement; disruptive behaviour; school disorganisation; lack of commitment; friends involved in anti-social behaviour; early involvement in anti-social behaviour; no skills or qualifications; unemployment orlow income; homelessness
Safer neighbourhoods	Improved security Improved design Improved housing services Preventive policing Community involvement	Opportunities for crime; availability of drugs; community disorganisation; high child density; transient population; early involvement in anti-social behaviour; friends involved in anti-social behaviour

crime and anti-social behaviour may decide to focus its attention on youth work projects, community policing and action to address truancy and exclusion. An area with a high rate of domestic burglary will prioritise domestic security measures, focused community policing and, if the offenders are young and local, diversionary measures to reduce their offending. An area with a high proportion of one parent households, children on the child protection register and behavioural problems in pre-school and primary schools will concentrate on early childhood preventive measures such as parenting training and family support.

The most successful programmes in high crime areas will be those which are able to implement a customised package of measures drawing on all three themes. As has been noted, the impact of a number of interventions is often greater than an additive model would suggest and protective factors have a stronger effect when more than one is present. Although this may create some organisational difficulties (see chapter four), it does mean that responsibility for prevention is shared among a number of agencies and budgets.

Many of the measures listed above are not, of course, 'crime prevention' measures and some may feel that including them within a framework to prevent crime and criminality plunders professional disciplines whose main purpose is unconnected with crime. Social policy therefore becomes crime-led. This is an understandable concern and deserves a response. There are four points to be made.

First, the real world does not neatly correspond with the boundaries of professional and academic disciplines. All the preventive measures listed can have a direct or indirect impact on offending and, where appropriate, should be enlisted to help prevent it.

Second, the main purpose of some of these measures is to support families and enhance opportunities for young people. At the same time, they may reduce the risk factors associated with offending, anti-social behaviour, school disruption and drug abuse. They can, therefore, have multiple benefits. This is a strength, not a weakness.

Third, and most important, measures such as pre-school education or youth work only impact on offending if they incorporate 'preventive mechanisms' within their design. Their potential to prevent offending must therefore be made explicit if it is to be realised (see chapter four).

Finally, demonstrating they can impact on crime increases their capacity to attract resources because the added benefits obtained from reduced offending may outweigh the costs of providing or increasing the service. In some cases, it may be preferable to present the approach as one concerned with the welfare of children and families or with opportunities for young people or with regeneration, rather than with crime and criminality (see, for example, the account of the strategy of the Dutch government described in chapter five). Nevertheless, when the reduction of crime is one of the main objectives, it has to be planned for and will not be achieved automatically as a result of funding youth projects or training initiatives.

To summarise, the geographical focus of this approach is the residential neighbourhood, its schools and its businesses.[60] Its target population group is children and young people at risk and their families. Its aim is to make crime more difficult to commit; to prevent drug misuse, anti-social behaviour and minor crime by children and young people; and to reduce the number who go on to become intermediate and persistent offenders. It also complements the efforts of criminal justice agencies to prevent re-offending by known young offenders. We will now turn to the three themes that form the basis of a local programme.

Early childhood prevention

There are clear links between early childhood experiences and later offending and there is increasing evidence that interventions can be successful. The main aims of early childhood services are not to reduce criminality but rather to enhance physical, intellectual and emotional development, to reduce child abuse and to improve family functioning. Frequently, these programmes have many positive benefits. They are advocated here because they can also reduce some of the risk factors associated with later offending. In addition, there is increasing interest in the early prevention of crime because of the limited success of remedial education and training programmes targeted at adolescent and young adult offenders.

Many people are not comfortable discussing 'interventions' in the family. Some feel that the family should be protected from government intervention and, in any case, there is little that government can do to improve the functioning of 'dysfunctional' families. Others believe that to consider the role of the family in delinquency and crime involves making value judgements about what constitutes good parenting and attributing blame to families when it ought to be directed elsewhere.

However, we know that certain types of childrearing are more likely to propel children into delinquency than others. We know that family discord and stress and low income are linked with higher rates of delinquency. We know that governments cannot avoid pursuing policies which support or damage the capacity of the family to be a good nurturing unit. It makes sense, therefore, to try to identify the policies that will support parents in the difficult task of childrearing, particularly when there are grounds for believing that high quality early prevention programmes may be effective at reducing later delinquency.[61]

Family-based programmes are also necessary because of non-reversible changes to the structure and functions of the modern family that have occurred in the post-war period. These have been caused by changes in the labour market and the nature of work, demands by women for the same opportunities as men, and the growth of consumerism. They have had a number of far-reaching consequences for the viability of the family (however defined) and the socialisation of children.

First, there has been a very rapid increase in the number of women working outside the home, a necessity for most households wishing to maintain a moderate level of income. Second, there has been an increase in the proportion of marriages that end in divorce (now levelling off at about 50 per cent). Third, there has been an increase in the number of one parent families. Fourth, increasing mobility has weakened extended family and community ties, cut off many parents from social networks and led to high levels of social isolation. Therefore, it is more difficult than it used to be for the family to raise children successfully. Those families without the resources to overcome these difficulties need support in the form of preventive family services.

Preventive services in early childhood include prenatal and infant development, family support, parental training and pre-school education and child care. Family and parent support programmes vary according to the intensity of the service being provided and can be classified as follows:

- *Universal services:* available to anyone wanting to make the most of being a parent
- *Neighbourhood services:* targeted at disadvantaged neighbourhoods and families under stress
- *Family preservation:* targeted at individual families in crisis which have come to the attention of social services or the police.[62]

Evaluations of preventive services in early childhood (mainly American) are most encouraging. They show that quality services for disadvantaged children can improve parenting and family functioning, reduce family breakdown and out of home care and improve the developmental and educational performance of young children.[63] Three will be examined here: family support programmes, parenting programmes and pre-school education.

Family support programmes
As we have seen, the family has not only become smaller, it has also become more socially isolated. Families subject to stress from whatever source now have less access to the informal support necessary to help them cope effectively. All families need support and many are able to obtain it from extended family and friends. Some can purchase it. Those at greatest risk are those which are poor and socially isolated.

If support is not forthcoming to families which are both socially isolated and multi-stressed, serious consequences can follow. A substantial body of research demonstrates that unsupported young mothers may become hostile and indifferent and reject their children; that socially isolated families are associated with high levels of abuse, neglect and later delinquency; and that children raised by a socially isolated parent living alone are more likely to fail school at an early age, truant from school, fight in school, drop out of school and become delinquent.[64]

Support can come in the form of intensive programmes for families in crisis, less intensive support for families in difficulty and parenting programmes for all parents. Intensive family support programmes in the United States claim to achieve substantial reductions in foster care and other out of home placements. They have helped to improve family functioning, children's school performance and parental employment; to increase parental self-esteem; to reduce child abuse and neglect; to reduce family size and to help families make better use of services and facilities. With regard to cost effectiveness, they estimate that there is a return of between $5 and $6 on every $1 invested because of reduced long-term foster care, group care or psychiatric hospitalisation.[65]

The direct impact of family support programmes on the future delinquency of children has not yet been demonstrated by longitudinal studies. However, since we know that delinquency is associated with family discord and breakdown, strengthening families, reducing out of home placements and improving the quality of parenting might reasonably be expected to influence children's later offending patterns.

One of the best known family support programmes in the UK is Homestart. Trained volunteers are used to support the families of preschool children. The aim is to prevent family breakdown. Volunteers visit twice a week and help to build up parents' confidence and skills so they can cope more effectively. A four year evaluation found that 86 per cent of the children registered at risk stayed out of care (although it was not possible to say with certainty that this was due to Homestart) and confirmed the beneficial change brought about by the programme.[66]

Parenting programmes

There is currently much interest in programmes set up with the explicit aim of improving parenting. Most parents want to be good parents but some lack the confidence and skills to do the job effectively. Parenting programmes can provide them with this support. American research shows that they can improve parenting, reduce child abuse and neglect, improve school achievement and reduce delinquency.[67]

Parenting programmes should be voluntary, sensitively delivered in a non-stigmatising way and culturally appropriate. The best ones concentrate on building up parents' capacities to be 'good enough' parents through enhancing their confidence and ability to deal with common parenting problems. In the UK, they are often based in neighbourhood family centres or around pre-schools or primary schools and may be linked to literacy projects. Many of these, including those located in disadvantaged areas, have shown real promise in terms of both improved parental confidence and improved behaviour and academic performance of children in school. Often, they may not be called 'parenting programmes' but improving parenting may be one of their key goals.

Of course, such measures are more likely to yield their full potential when accompanied by action to alleviate at least some of the outside stresses – such as poverty and unemployment – which make it more difficult to be a 'good enough' parent. Nevertheless, there is evidence that they can make a measurable difference to the quality of parenting. An evaluation found that 90 per cent of the 10,000 parents who completed Parent Network's Parent Link thirteen week course felt more confident and said they had learned new skills. Seventy per cent said they had observed significant improvements in their children's behaviour.[68]

A recent study by the Joseph Rowntree Foundation revealed that although group-based parenting programmes have grown over the past five to ten years in the UK, under 30,000 parents attend them.[69] The majority who do attend are white, middle class mothers with young children. Yet the public believes that more responsible parenting is a priority for reducing criminality.[70] There is also evidence of a significant demand for it, at least among those who shop in a well-known supermarket: 60 per cent of the 14,000 parents responding to a survey in *Sainsbury's Magazine* said they would welcome parenting courses if they were available.[71] In a survey of organisations running parenting programmes, 60 per cent reported heavy demand.[72] More demonstration projects are needed to assess what works best for those parents who most need support.

Pre-school education

High quality pre-school education can help disadvantaged children by raising achievement and self-esteem and improving social skills. Again, US studies show that it can engender a culture of personal success which is subsequently reflected in performance in primary and secondary school, future career patterns and relatively low arrest rates.

The frequently cited High/Scope Perry Pre-school Programme is one of the few to have looked at the link between pre-school education and the inhibition of delinquency. This programme strikingly demonstrates the potential benefits of high quality early childhood programmes for poor children. It shows convincingly that pre-school participation can increase the proportion of young people who at age nineteen are literate, employed and enrolled in post-secondary education, and can reduce the proportion who drop out of school, have been arrested or are on welfare.[73] By age 27, the experimental group had accumulated only half as many arrests as the control group.[74]

An economic cost-benefit analysis of the Perry Pre-school Programme and its long-term effects revealed that such a programme can be an excellent investment for tax payers, returning $6 for every $1 invested in a one year programme and $3 for every $1 invested in a two year programme.[75] Other research on good early childhood programmes has demonstrated positive short-term and long-term results.[76]

It should be noted that not all pre-school activity is necessarily preventive. The key features of the approaches cited here are systematic efforts to involve parents as partners in their children's learning, a curriculum based on child-initiated learning, classes with two adults and fewer than twenty children and teachers trained in early childhood development. Encouraging children to plan and then take responsibility for their activities within a structured classroom environment is considered especially important for delinquency prevention because it is believed that active learners will be more community minded and responsible in adolescence.[77]

There is a strong tradition of good pre-school education in the UK and it is probable that many pre-school education facilities have achieved similar benefits to those achieved by the successful demonstration programmes in the United States. The High/Scope curriculum is not necessarily the only route to quality and preventive effectiveness. It has been described in some detail because it is one of the very few that has been concerned with delinquency prevention and that has been rigorously evaluated. One UK pre-school project worth mentioning is the Moulsecoombe Playlink Project in Brighton which serves children aged between one and a half and three years. Research found that participating children had improved self-confidence and social and educational skills on arrival at nursery school.[78] More research of this type on UK pre-school provision is needed to fill the many gaps in our knowledge and to determine the preventive impact of early years education.

We do know, however, that there are not enough affordable, good quality services and that disadvantaged children in the UK are proportionately less likely to attend a pre-school facility.[79] One survey found that nearly half of the most disadvantaged children had received no pre-school education compared with only 10 per cent of the most advantaged group.[80] We also know that pre-school education in the UK varies widely and that the children who are most at risk do not, by and large, attend the facilities which are likely to offer them the best advantages. Although all types of well managed pre-school provision are good for children,[81] disadvantaged children would probably benefit more from provision which combines care with a structured educational content and a significant level of parental involvement.[82]

In the judgement of one researcher, it is possible to argue with some confidence that educationally-orientated pre-school programmes can prevent educational and behavioural problems later in life, that the children in the UK who are most at risk of behavioural and intellectual problems should attend day nursery care provision run by local authority social services departments, and that there is an urgent need to improve educational provision in day nurseries if the life chances of disadvantaged children are to be improved.[83]

Some of the research suggests that the intellectual (though not social) benefits of pre-school can diminish over time and the mechanism by which pre-school education is thought to achieve its long-term effect requires a degree of subsequent reinforcement in both the home and the school. This will be discussed in the next section.

Summary: early childhood prevention
The value of preventive services has long been recognised in the UK by the major children's charities, social services professionals and organisations such as Newpin, Homesafe and the Family Centre movement.

Unfortunately, there has not been the same commitment to evaluation as in the United States. In addition, the resources of the statutory sector in the UK have been engaged almost exclusively in child protection work although this is now beginning to change. Most preventive work has been provided through neighbourhood family centres run by large voluntary child care organisations, often jointly with social services departments.

Many of these provide valuable support services in areas of great need. However, apart from the general shortage of provision, there are significant gaps in the preventive jigsaw. While those who are most at risk come to the attention of the statutory services, only a small proportion of the families in a locality might contact their family centre in any one year and only about one in four of the most disadvantaged families use them.[84] Furthermore, there is little provision for those who are in difficulty but who have not yet come to the attention of the statutory services.

A determined effort is needed to improve the quality of preventive services. First, more and better preventive services are required in order to reach the majority of those who most need them. Second, intensive services aimed at strengthening families under stress are required to prevent matters deteriorating to the point that they come to the attention of the social services department. Third, more attention should be paid to monitoring and evaluating interventions; at present, we do not know very much about the effectiveness of the various forms of preventive family work undertaken in the UK. Fourth, preventive work needs to be given a much higher status. As we have seen, evaluations of successful American programmes suggest that preventive services targeted at families with young children can have many short-term and long-term benefits.

Most important, for the purposes of this book, is their capacity to reduce some of the risk factors associated with anti-social behaviour and offending. There is a great need for more preventive family services in Britain, a view endorsed in the 1989 Children Act, a 1993 Audit Commission report and in the under-eights reviews and children's services plans of many local authorities.[85] It is also a view expressed by many residents in disadvantaged areas and by the recipients of the services.

Opportunities for young people

There is increasing acceptance that much more attention needs to be paid to pre-school education because, to quote Alexander Pope, 'as the twig is bent, so's the tree inclined'. Others argue that this view can be taken too far and that is wrong to suppose that early childhood experiences are always decisive and critical.[86] The early years are especially important because what happens then may start a chain of events leading into later life, but if early preventive experience is to have a permanent effect, it must be subsequently reinforced and built on.[87] Hence good pre-school education must be followed by good primary and secondary education and services aimed at diverting young people from crime through youth work and housing, training and employment opportunities.

School improvement

Research has shown clearly that pupils, especially boys, who under-perform or fail at school are more likely to become involved in anti-social and delinquent activities than those who succeed. Factors which contribute to school failure, such as disaffection, bullying behaviour, poor attendance and disruptive behaviour, therefore also increase the risk of a young person becoming delinquent.[88]

Behaviour, attendance and performance at school are affected by many factors, some of which lie outside the control of the school. The home has been seen as the single most influential factor in children's development and many writers have observed that 'schools cannot compensate for society'. Indeed, until relatively recently it was widely thought that schools could do little about students who fail or behave disruptively or truant and that these problems were largely due to individual students and their family backgrounds.

There is a weight of evidence, however, which suggests strongly that the school itself also has considerable impact on young people. Even when the catchment area and home background of students is taken into account, researchers have found significant differences between schools in terms of the proportion of their students who behave anti-socially and offend.[89] Some schools in high crime areas have relatively low delinquency rates while others in low crime areas have high rates.

This suggests that schools are able to exert an independent influence on student behaviour both within and, sometimes, outside of the school.

While it is difficult to demonstrate a direct causal relationship between schools and delinquency, schools can affect levels of delinquency indirectly by the strong and direct effects they have on disruptive behaviour, truancy and school failure which are themselves associated with delinquency. Schools which are able to offer all students a sense of achievement regardless of ability and are able to motivate and integrate them are likely to reduce problems such as school failure and delinquency. The most effective schools enjoy high quality leadership and relations between members of the school community, ongoing staff development, a positive ethos, high expectations, clear goals, enthusiasm among staff and students, a breadth of vision, delegation, responsiveness to the needs of the community, parents and governors, and a problem solving approach to change.[90]

Similarly, schools which are likely to have high rates of delinquency are those which segregate pupils rigidly according to academic ability, concentrate on academic success at the expense of practical and social skills, categorise pupils as failures and tend to refer responsibility for the behaviour and welfare of their pupils to outside agencies. Schools which permanently exclude their most difficult pupils or ignore those who persistently fail to attend school may themselves be contributing to the promotion of delinquency.[91]

The 'school effect' can be seen in the results of one study which found that children of the same ability would get a CSE grade 3 in English in one school and an O level grade B in another. The differences between schools, it is argued, are not as great as the differences between the homes of their pupils and effective schools are not going to compensate for the enormous differences between individual pupils in terms of ability and motivation. However, the 'school effect' appears to be substantial enough to 'ratchet' up the level of educational achievement in a school and make a significant difference to the life chances of children. For some, this will increase their motivation to succeed and lead to reduced disruption, truancy and delinquency. The authors argue that if all schools were improved only within the current range of performance of urban comprehensive schools, this would be enough to transform the standard of secondary education.[92]

It is worth noting that in the UK many school-based interventions have been evaluated. Some have consistently demonstrated positive effects on risk and protective factors for delinquency. The most important include reduced class size for pre-school and primary reception classes; classroom behaviour management techniques; rigorous monitoring of behaviour, attendance and progress; and parenting training skills. Other approaches have not been evaluated but are thought to be sufficiently promising to warrant further research. Yet others may not have much of an impact on delinquency but may have other benefits.[93]

In addition to generally improving their management and effectiveness, there are more specific measures which schools can take to reduce the risks of anti-social behaviour and delinquency directly. These include:

- preventing truancy
- reducing exclusions
- stimulating parental interest
- encouraging peer education initiatives
- preventing bullying
- broadening the curriculum.

Preventing truancy. Young people who persistently fail to attend school are more likely to offend than regular attendees. A 1991 TVAM investigation found that as many as 200,000 young people regularly go absent from school, 500,000 skip lessons frequently and one half of year eleven students in inner city schools truant.[94] Twenty per cent of schools admit a problem of serious truancy.[95] A 1995 report found that 37 per cent of males and 28 per cent of females said they had skipped school for at least one day without permission. It calculated that truants were three times more likely to offend than those who had not truanted. Those who persistently truanted were even more likely to admit to offending: 78 per cent of males and 53 per cent of females who truanted once a week admitted offending.[96]

There are many measures that schools can adopt to help integrate those most at risk of offending – the persistent truants, the failures, the most troublesome. Special reintegration programmes can be devised to coax school refusers back into school. Locally based teams of peripatetic teachers skilled in work with difficult children should be made available to schools to help them resolve problems of disruptive behaviour within the school or the classroom at the earliest possible stage.

In some cases, schools may need to review their own organisation and 'ethos' with a view to changing any internal conditions which might give rise to truancy and disruptive behaviour.[97] Additionally, many non-attendees do not have access to a quiet place in their home to do their homework. In such cases, the school can provide rooms in which homework may be done after school. Such provision will reduce children's anxiety about completing work at home against competing demands and this is likely to have a beneficial effect on their motivation to attend school.[98]

In both the United States and UK, the Cities in Schools (CiS) project is bringing intensive care to young people whose personal attitudes to education and difficult social circumstances prevent them from obtaining the start in life which they deserve. They do this through improving school attendance, increasing parental involvement in the education of their children, improving students' self-esteem and developing their personal and social skills, thereby contributing to their chances of future employment or further education. CiS also coordinates the provision available for vulnerable young people and their families.

The project's 1993-94 Bridge Course (for fifteen to sixteen year olds) led to an increase in positive attitudes to education from 45 per cent to 91 per cent of its participants and improved attendance from 42 per cent to 87 per cent. Seventy six per cent of its students moved into further education, training and employment.[99]

Reducing exclusion. Of particular importance in any debate about youth offending is the issue of exclusion. There has been a threefold increase in the number of pupils excluded from school since 1991-92, coinciding with the introduction of the 1993 Education Act which introduced 'league tables' and, in effect, increased competition between schools. In 1994-95, over 11,000 pupils were excluded.[100] These young people often receive only the statutory minimum three sessions of education per week. For the rest of the week (and sometimes for the whole week while they are waiting to be allocated a place at an out-of-school centre), they are free to roam the streets. Excluded young people are much more likely to admit to offending and other anti-social behaviour.[101]

More support for schools is necessary to reduce the use of exclusion. For those who are excluded, there should be fast allocation to an out-of-school facility which should develop a systematic plan for returning the young people to full-time education or training. There should also be a comprehensive response to the predicament of the excludees and their families. This might include home visits, youth service support during the day and voluntary education or mentoring schemes (see for example the Dalston Youth Project described on page 64).

Other ideas include a requirement for schools to transfer first time excludees to another school (on a quid pro quo basis); extra funds to help schools accommodate pupils who are at risk of being excluded; use of low exclusion rates as a performance indicator; and more flexible use of further education colleges and work experience programmes for fifteen to sixteen year olds. However, many excludees (and many young people generally) are demotivated by the perception that there are no jobs for them. This issue is addressed later in this chapter.

Stimulating parental interest. One of the most significant 'protective' factors found in the backgrounds of children from economically disadvantaged homes whose attainment is above average is a parent who displays a keen interest in their education. Programmes that focus on improving the interest of parents in their children's education from the earliest years may play a major role in reducing the risk of later school failure. Involving parents in their children's education is, of course, easier at pre-school and primary school level than at secondary school.

The conditions for high attendance are set when the school manages the induction of new pupils skilfully and explains its policies to parents carefully. Many schools have home-school contracts and some have set up home-school councils. In areas of ethnic diversity, schools have made extensive use of community leaders in liaising with parents. Some schools offer clear guidelines on the role parents can play in helping children with their homework; this can reduce the likelihood of failure to undertake such assignments being an excuse for not attending school.[102] In one secondary school in south London, teachers have visited the parents of all the students in their homes in order to emphasise the importance of parental interest.

In the section on early childhood prevention, the benefits of parenting programmes were described. Surprisingly, there are few sources of advice for the parents of older children. Adolescence is the age when children can be most difficult to supervise. The average age of onset for offending, drug misuse and running away from home is thirteen to fourteen. In addition to the help that might be provided by, say, schools and open access family centres, more specialist services may be needed to help the parents of teenagers, perhaps modelled on the Homestart family support project and using experienced parents as volunteers. This is particularly important since poor parental supervision is linked to truancy and both are linked to offending.

Peer group activities. Since the influence of parents diminishes as children grow up and is replaced by that of their peers, it makes sense to consider how such influence can be used to positive effect. Many schools find ways of involving their pupils in the life of the school and, in some cases, give them significant levels of responsibility. For example, the headteacher of a comprehensive school in Tyneside argues that the key to eliminating crime and vandalism in school is by involving pupils in planning improvements to the school, including spending decisions. Under Local Management of Schools, he gave his pupils responsibility for spending £200,000 via a committee on which each class has a representative. The cost of vandalism has been reduced by 75 per cent during the three years following the introduction of the scheme and the pupils were able to spend the money saved on whatever they wished.[103]

Many schools are also using peer-led education techniques to educate young people about drug misuse although the effectiveness of this approach has yet to be definitively established.[104]

Preventing bullying. Effective schools will, by and large, have low levels of bullying and all schools should have a clear policy which is firmly enforced. Apart from the very damaging impact bullying has on victims, a significant proportion of bullies go on to become adult offenders. Many schools have anti-bullying strategies and some excellent materials for teachers have been produced. Some also organise conflict resolution and violence prevention courses. The anti-bullying initiative which the Department for Education and Employment has supported in Sheffield and endorsed for wider replication promotes a 'whole school' response to the problem.[105]

Broadening the curriculum. The 1988 Education Act lays a duty on schools to provide a broad and balanced curriculum which equips young people for life. This, of course, includes those pupils who are not academically strong or who have special educational needs. There is still no professional consensus on what should constitute an effective alternative to the academic curriculum for such pupils. As a result, talented pupils with less academic strengths can, in some schools, find it difficult to gain the self-esteem and sense of achievement which is a precondition of good behaviour in school and 'school success'.

Some have argued that the GCSE examination makes it difficult for schools to motivate the disaffected or less able. This examination, it is argued, is highly competitive, with only 30 to 40 per cent of the age group achieving high grades in five or more subjects. Managing this situation creates problems for urban schools which have to organise themselves around the requirements of the exam system (with testing at years seven, eleven, fourteen and sixteen) because a large proportion of pupils will be confronted with failure for much of their secondary school career. This is considered to be demotivating and wasteful of talent.[106] In the UK, up to a half of young people leave at the earliest opportunity, their attitudes to education soured by their experience of the examination system.

This drop-out rate (which is much higher than that of many other countries) results in a high level of educational underachievement and is almost certainly a contributor to both juvenile and adult offending. It is not inevitable. An evaluation of the Technical and Vocational Educational Initiative found that young people value practical activities, problem solving approaches and greater access to high quality information technology.[107] The school curriculum needs to be broadened to take account of this finding and to enable a far larger proportion of our young people to succeed in school.

Many schools and LEAs have, of course, taken positive steps to achieve success in this area, often under very difficult circumstances, not least those concerning increased competition stimulated by parental choice and the publication of league tables. Eleven of these are reviewed in the 1996 report by the National Commission on Education, *Success against the odds*, which concluded that 'all schools, regardless of their situation, can not only be successful but can go on improving year after year'. Those which have not yet achieved this goal will need support and resources if their contribution to reducing crime and anti-social behaviour is to be realised.

Youth work

In addition to school-based prevention, youth projects which are able to occupy young people constructively in their neighbourhoods are essential. Research shows that children and young people who have a lot of unsupervised leisure time which they spend with their friends are more likely to behave anti-socially and drift into crime.[108] Much petty crime and anti-social behaviour could be prevented by making available recreational, sporting and social activities supported by skilled staff able to motivate and involve young people. In addition, there is also a need for more focused work with those young people who are or who may become persistent offenders.

Unfortunately, it has so far not been possible to demonstrate unequivocally that youth work prevents youth crime.[109] There are a number of explanations for this. Firstly, many youth programmes do not include delinquency prevention as one of their main objectives. In the UK, many youth workers see their mission as social education; they wish to provide a non-stigmatising, voluntary service and are generally unwilling to develop too close a relationship with the police. Consequently, the potential of youth work to reduce juvenile offending, although acknowledged by some youth workers, may not have been realised in practice because it never became a sufficiently important objective.[110] There are signs, fortunately, that this may be changing.

Secondly, only a minority of young people currently use youth service provision in the UK. The areas with the highest concentrations of youth crime are, paradoxically, those which are often least well covered by youth work programmes. Where they do exist, they are sometimes poorly funded, weakly managed and exhausted by their efforts to support young people with very difficult problems.

Thirdly, in many areas, there is a mismatch between what is needed and what is on offer. For example, organised clubs and activities are best for under-fourteens, but in many areas the youth service does not cater for younger children. Older young people often prefer commercial facilities and drop-in centres where they can organise their own activities, rather than 'traditional' youth clubs.

Outreach or detached youth work, aimed at contacting and involving young people most at risk of offending, is essential but there is far too little of it. Counselling and advice services can provide young people with the support they are unable or unwilling to seek within their own networks but these are not widely available. It is salutary to remember that some areas no longer have a youth service and many others are only able to make minimum provision. In inner London, it has been estimated that youth service resources have been reduced by 80 per cent since the mid 1980s.

Nevertheless, many partnerships, local authorities and voluntary youth organisations are trying to develop innovative responses to the problems facing young people and their communities. Some areas have developed city-wide or town-wide youth crime prevention strategies. An audit assesses local problems by collating crime-related data and consulting the community, local agencies and young people. Its purpose is to clarify the nature of the problems (anti-social behaviour, bullying, car crime, burglary, drug misuse), the age group responsible and the type of tried and tested responses that local adult residents, young people and agencies think will work in their neighbourhood. Here, there is a coordinated response to the problem, resources are directed to high crime areas and local preventive initiatives are developed. There are two main types of project.

The first is mainstream play, recreational and youth provision in the form of staffed playgrounds (fixed equipment, adventure); junior and senior youth clubs; summer holiday activity schemes; and children's centres. The extent to which this provision impacts on anti-social behaviour and offending depends to a large extent on where it is located, how often it operates, how it is managed and whether it targets those most at risk of offending. At its best, such provision can make a significant impact on minor youth crime and related problems and is highly valued by young people and their parents.

Second, there are projects set up to address particular concerns such as persistent offending, drug misuse or racially motivated crime. They have explicit objectives and carefully thought out strategies to achieve them. Outreach or detached workers may be employed to engage with those who are most at risk of doing harm to themselves and others. Drop-in centres may be established as a base for such contact. Examples include peer-led education to tackle drug and alcohol abuse; training and employment programmes, youth-community mediation schemes; and housing, counselling and advice services. Emphasis is placed on involving young people closely in the planning of initiatives, engaging with those most likely to offend and liaising with relevant agencies to ensure that services for young people are coordinated.

Because there have been few youth work programmes to date with an explicit focus on preventing crime and even fewer which have been evaluated, we do not know as much as we need to about the types of provision which are most likely to be effective. Many believe that youth agencies could play a bigger role in the prevention of delinquency without compromising the principles of youth work by focusing resources on areas with high concentrations of young people at risk, ensuring these young people are targeted, using outreach youth workers, working with other agencies to tackle the range of issues that may concern young people (such as drugs, family problems and employment) and specifying aims and objectives more precisely.[111]

The potential of youth work to prevent offending can be illustrated by four projects. The first is the Bristol SPLASH scheme organised by the police and other agencies on the Southmead estate in the north of the city in the summer of 1992. This included a programme of sports and other recreational activity for 250 young people aged ten to sixteen; outdoor pursuits away from the estate involving 25 young people at risk of offending; and a social services family project for seventeen young people at risk of offending or 'beyond parental control'. In addition to the summer activity programme, the estate benefited from door and window security improvements, new fencing and gates and external security lighting.

Recorded crime fell by 29 per cent during the summer activity period in July and August 1992, compared with the same period in 1991. The sharpest reductions were in domestic burglary (down 64 per cent) and theft from motor vehicles (down 68 per cent). Housing department repair orders were also down 50 per cent compared with the same period in 1991. The summer activity programme was repeated in 1994, and a further 20 per cent reduction in crime was recorded. The reductions were attributable to both the security improvements and the youth activity scheme.[112]

The second, a detached youth work project, was set up on the Castlefields estate in Runcorn by Crime Concern and the Cheshire County Council Youth Service to reduce anti-social behaviour and improve relationships between young people and the wider community. It enabled young people to find constructive solutions to their problems and reduced the incidence of anti-social behaviour and petty crime. Altogether, ten different groups and activities were developed, involving 50 to 60 young people. A 1994 evaluation of the project found that calls to the police attributable to rowdy youths on the estate declined by 57 per cent between January 1993 and 1994. In addition, it created an opportunity for the young people to make a significant contribution to the community by undertaking a lighting survey which led to the repair of streetlamps and the installation of 150 new lights in the area.[113]

The third project is Youthworks, a programme set up by Crime Concern, the Groundwork Foundation and Marks and Spencer on high crime estates in five cities. This combines measures to prevent youth crime with those aimed at improving the estate environment. Young people work with local agencies to plan improvements and develop activities for young people, often using the 'Planning for Real' approach in which residents plan improvements to their neighbourhood using models constructed by architects. In some cases, 'older' young people have been recruited and trained to become volunteer youth workers. These projects are beginning to reduce crime and behaviour problems: a housing association responsible for the estate in Blackburn on which one of the projects is located has reported a significant reduction in vandalism which it attributes to the project. Furthermore, the projects have captured the interest of local agencies in a way that youth projects have rarely been able to do. In Leeds, the council want to replicate the approach developed in the Beeston area to other parts of the city.

The fourth project is the Dalston Youth Project, an education and mentoring project in Hackney, east London. It works with young people aged fifteen to eighteen who are offenders, have been excluded from school or are persistent truants. The project aims to help young people turn their lives around, away from offending and towards positive goals related to education, vocational attainment and personal development. The three components are a week long residential course to help young people decide their objectives, an education and training programme to provide them with the skills to achieve them and an attachment to an adult volunteer mentor for one year to provide them with the necessary support.

A comparison of arrest rates for 25 of the young people in the project's first cohort for the year before and the year of involvement found reductions of between 50 and 70 per cent, according to the level of participation, and sixteen young people enrolled on college or training courses. Moreover, the evaluation judged the project to be cost effective, that is, the estimated cost of the number of crimes prevented amounted to a greater value than the cost of the project.[114] A school-based project to prevent eleven to fourteen year olds being excluded has been established recently in two of the borough's secondary schools.

The mentoring element is of particular interest. Mentoring provides a form of supervision and constitutes 'parenting at a distance' which has been recommended for young people after they have left home.[115] It may be particularly valuable in helping young men to desist from offending, especially if they have been in care or have no relationships with stable, mature adults.

Drug misuse is though to be a major cause of offending. However, both drug misuse and offending may be part of a particular lifestyle and preventing drug misuse will not necessarily prevent offending, although it may reduce the volume of crime committed. The two problems need to be tackled together. The risk factors associated with serious drug misuse are, by and large, those which can also lead to persistent criminality. Many of the preventive measures advocated in this book will reduce both offending and drug misuse. Duplication and waste will result if separate preventive strategies are introduced. At a local level, a single multi-agency group should be responsible for preventing both problems.

Specific measures to reduce drug misuse will involve police action to reduce supply; services for drug users such as substitute prescribing, needle exchange and counselling; advice for young people; and preventive education work in schools, including peer-led initiatives such as those which have been piloted in Solihull and Newham. Alcohol misuse is often to linked to violent crime (rather than property crime to fund an expensive habit) and can be reduced by a range of measures from training for licensees and bar staff, and restrictions on the sale to juveniles to education programmes in schools and youth clubs. Many of these approaches have been taken forward by the government's much-praised Tackling Drugs Together programme and the establishment of Drug Action Teams.

In devising local plans to tackle drug misuse, anti-social behaviour and youth crime, town and neighbourhood forums should be considered to allow for an exchange of views between young people and the adult community. These can lead to greater mutual understanding among sections of the community who rarely meet one another and can help reduce some of the problems that stem from a poor relationship and lack of communication.

More opportunities are also needed to help mature young people become youth workers. Most youth work courses require educational qualifications as a condition of selection. These are a barrier to many young people who have grown up in high crime areas and who would be very good youth workers capable of using their firsthand experience to divert the next generation from crime.

Training and employment
The relationship between crime and unemployment is a complex one but common sense suggests that young people who are unemployed or underemployed are at greater risk of offending than those who are not. Three quarters of a sample of sixteen to seventeen year olds

attending youth courts were not in education, training or employment.[116] Nationally, between 5 and 10 per cent of young people under 25 are not in education, training or employment and cannot be tracked down. In many areas, this figure will be much higher.[117] Many young people have no contact with any service which may be able help them.

Considerable reductions in the number of adequately paid semi-skilled and unskilled jobs over the past two decades have made it more difficult for some young people, especially young men, without qualifications to avoid drugs, crime and a lifestyle based on underemployment. These young people are unprepared to compete in a changing jobs market. They need help if they are to have a chance of succeeding in the future.

Failure to help vulnerable young people into training and work will result in increased reliance on benefits, reduced tax revenues and increased criminal activity. High unemployment among young men and falling wages also threaten family formation which in turn results in larger proportions of children being born into poor, one parent households.

There are four main ways of tackling this issue at a local level. The first is to provide quality training programmes. At present, youth training scheme providers get paid by results, based on the number of young people who subsequently get qualifications or jobs. Therefore many existing youth training schemes aim for a high quality intake and are unlikely to select the young people who are most at risk of offending. The key features of training initiatives aimed at young people at risk are that they actively target difficult young people; they recognise that these young people may not be equipped or motivated to compete for a government-sponsored youth training place; and they provide education opportunities to redress their social and educational disadvantages.

The second approach is to encourage companies who have won contracts – especially on regeneration projects – to advertise for, and employ and train, local labour. Although Compulsory Competitive Tendering rules do not permit local labour to be specified, it is possible to ask tenderers to state how they intend to recruit employees. In Dalston, east London, the main City Challenge building contractors have provided skill training for local young people on the targeted estates prior to hiring labour.

Another aim of many area improvement strategies is to attract new employment opportunities into the area in the longer term. What frequently happens however is that the new jobs require skills levels not available locally or that employers move into the area bringing their existing workforce with them. In any event, area improvement strategies are likely to provide jobs for the most employable and best qualified young people locally, who are probably not those most at risk. A major opportunity to benefit young people at risk is often lost unless specific attention is paid to this issue.

The third approach is to encourage the private sector to participate in local regeneration schemes such as the One Stop Shops promoted by the Department for Education and Employment through the Priority Estates Project. One Stop Shops can offer a range of economic regeneration services, such as enterprise promotion, advice on setting up community controlled businesses, job placement and advice on skills training. The aim is to provide a route to employment via basic skills training, work skills training, work experience and counselling and support. The private sector can finance or sponsor skills audits, help provide training, guarantee jobs to local people, offer business advice, help manage workshops, contribute managerially and financially to regeneration programmes and make premises available.

The fourth is to encourage entrepreneurship. This includes advice on community business strategies, provision of self-employed start-up grants and training. However, such schemes are more likely to benefit skilled and confident young people than marginal youth in high crime areas.[118]

Many eighteen to 25 year olds find it difficult to get a job because they have never had a job. The work of the WISE group suggests that what matters most in helping young people obtain work is the discipline of work experience. The 'intermediate labour market' programme provides young people with a job for a year. As a result, they gain a reference and work experience and are paid the rate for the job. This makes them more employable. An evaluation found that this approach could be very successful with marginalised young people, assisting 55 per cent of them into employment. In addition, the programme also ensures that work of value to the local community is undertaken.[119]

South Glamorgan Training and Enterprise Council has developed an innovative response – Action on Missing Youth – to the substantial number of young people aged sixteen to eighteen who are not in education, training or employment, estimated at between 16 and 23 per cent by one study. Twelve outreach workers have been deployed through the county to encourage young people to take part in training programmes. Particular importance is being given to ex-offenders and those with special needs.[120]

In the United States, research has found that programmes which focus on providing long-term, quality employment are more likely to be effective than those which simply try to change behaviour or only provide vocational advice or short-term employment. Initiatives which seriously address the depth and complexity of the problems faced by high risk populations can make a difference. Job Corps involved six month residential settings and a tough programme of education, skills training and health care and worked for a substantial number of participants. Graduates got better jobs, earned higher incomes and were less dependent on welfare. Every $1 invested in Job Corps returned $1.45 to the American taxpayer. Supported work programmes offer advice, counselling, training, real jobs and a working environment and are often necessary because high risk people need to be levered into the job market slowly and with support.[121]

Helping offenders and those at risk of offending into employment is likely to be one of the most effective ways of preventing criminality.

Homelessness
Similarly, helping vulnerable young people to find housing will help reduce the risk of them drifting into crime. Homelessness leads to a higher risk of involvement in, and victimisation of, crime. Young people in unstable accommodation admitted to substantially more offending than those in more stable housing.[122]

According to research commissioned by the Probation Service, 30 per cent of probation clients under 23 years of age left home before the age of sixteen, many having suffered abuse.[123] Centrepoint calculated a 35 per cent increase in London hostels in the under-nineteen age group between 1987 and 1992.[124] An estimated 200,000 to 300,000 young people become homeless every year.[125] Many of these will stay with friends or in other forms of transitory accommodation and will be invisible to the statutory agencies. Particularly at risk are young people leaving local authority care. Thirty per cent of Centrepoint's clients have been in foster care or in children's homes.[126]

Many projects tackling youth homelessness focus on young people 'in priority need', where there is a statutory obligation to help – for example, those leaving care or coming out of custodial institutions. There is, however, acknowledged to be a much larger group of young people at risk, hidden from official view.

There is a need for more provision of information and advice. Most housing departments and a number of voluntary organisations provide information and advice for homeless, single young people. Often this is limited to providing a list of names and addresses of private sector landlords. Some housing advice centres also help by guaranteeing a deposit to get round the housing-benefits trap facing homeless and jobless people. A few go even further, for example, the London Borough of Hackney publicises the right of all homeless young people aged sixteen and seventeen to receive help from the local authority under the 1989 Children Act.

Particular attention should be paid to young people leaving care or custody. Special efforts are required to ensure that they have adequate access to housing. Some local authorities have specialist leaving care teams and a quota of local authority housing. Group tenancies and other forms of house-share arrangements are rare, as local authorities continue to divest themselves of their housing stock and financial stringencies place more emphasis on those in even greater priority need, such as families with children.

Of special interest is the Foyer approach, introduced into this country from France by Shelter. This is a form of medium-term, shared accommodation for young people which encourages a strong sense of community plus access to training and employment opportunities, as a stepping stone from home to independence. Foyer schemes are now being developed in a number of areas in the UK and an organisation has been set up to promote them.

Summary: opportunities for young people
Enhancing opportunities for young people in the crucial areas of schooling, youth work, training, employment and housing can prevent them from drifting into crime in the first place or divert them from crime, drug misuse and anti-social behaviour and into more constructive activities.

Schooling can either inhibit or compound the delinquent predispositions of young people from vulnerable families. In addition to action to reduce truancy and exclusion, schools should be given more help to engage the disaffected and develop the interest of their parents in their children's education. Parent interest and heightened aspirations further encourage pupil success. Two key risk factors associated with anti-social behaviour and delinquency – parental disinterest in school and pupil school failure – are thereby directly addressed.

Recreational, sporting and social activities for children and young people can occupy them constructively and expose them to new interests and supportive adults. As a result, many will be diverted from anti-social behaviour and crime. Detached youth work can engage with those young people who are excluded or have excluded themselves from mainstream youth activities. Research shows how it can significantly reduce the harm they do to themselves and their community.

Access to training, employment and housing opportunities will enable older young people to develop the skills and confidence necessary to move from adolescence to adulthood successfully. In so doing, the risks of them offending or continuing to offend are significantly reduced. This is particularly important in the light of recent findings which show that many young male offenders are no longer growing out of crime as they enter early adulthood, as used to be the case.[127]

These approaches – early childhood prevention and opportunities for young people – are likely to be most effective in neighbourhoods where opportunities for crime have been reduced and tolerance of anti-social behaviour is low. How this might be achieved is the subject of the next section.

Safer neighbourhoods
It is at the neighbourhood level that social and situational crime prevention come together. Most of the measures advocated so far in

this book are aimed at reducing the predisposition of young people to offend through supporting and strengthening the family, increasing the effectiveness of schools and youth services and helping young people into employment (social crime prevention). These approaches are most likely to be successful if they are complemented by measures that make crime more difficult and risky and less rewarding to commit (situational crime prevention). This can be done by improving the security, design and management of neighbourhoods.

'Security' refers to the application of various security and surveillance devices to deter or prevent crime against homes, schools, shops and other businesses and community buildings. 'Design' refers to modifying buildings and the external layout of a neighbourhood or estate. It is discussed mainly in connection with some social housing estates, the design shortcomings of which are thought by many to exacerbate crime problems. 'Neighbourhood management' is concerned with the assessment of need, the provision of community services, the resolution of problems and the overall coordination of multi-agency activity. It is a concept that is broader than the management of particular services and can apply to mixed tenure neighbourhoods and estates managed by social landlords.

Improving the security, design and management of neighbourhoods, especially those which include a high proportion of social housing and vulnerable families, can help create an environment in which the supervision of the young (by parents and others) is more easily undertaken. In some circumstances, this can stimulate social cohesion and the informal controls which naturally check anti-social and petty criminal behaviour. In such neighbourhoods, children and young people quickly learn what they can and cannot do.

In areas where informal controls are weak, parents find it much more difficult to exercise control over their young because their efforts are not reinforced by the wider community. People are less likely to challenge the unacceptable behaviour of their neighbours' children. In the worst areas, a small number of families can pose a serious threat to order and stability. Any attempt to rebuild confidence in such communities must be led by those with the authority to resolve these difficult problems, acting with the support of the majority of residents. This will involve tackling the issues below.

Security

The first step is to ensure that dwellings, commercial properties, local schools, community buildings and public areas are made physically secure. Priority should be given to those who have already been victimised and those who are most at risk. Prevention measures may include:

- better locks and security fittings
- 'cocoon' neighbourhood watch
- improvements to boundary fencing and walls
- closure or locking of alleyways
- targeted preventive policing.

Targeting victims can be the most cost effective way of reducing the burglary rate. Some individuals and places are repeatedly victimised. Areas with high crime rates tend to have especially high rates of repeat victimisation. Repeat victimisations tend to occur quickly and the same offenders are often responsible. In some areas, a graded response has been devised according to the number of prior victimisations. For those victimised three or more times, more sophisticated measures to prevent the burglary can be coordinated with measures to detect the offender.[128]

The Kirkholt estate burglary prevention project in Rochdale and Crime Concern's Homesafe projects in seven Safer City areas are good examples of the targeted application of physical security measures in high crime locations. Both have led to substantial reductions in burglary and fear of crime and to an increase in community confidence.[129]

Design

Good security should be complemented by good design. Design improvements commonly applied to housing estates include the provision of front and rear gardens for conventionally designed houses and reductions in the amount of undesignated open space around them since this is often misused and considered unsafe by residents. Other design changes include improvements to lighting, road and pedestrian access, more secure car parking and increased opportunities for formal or informal surveillance.

Estates of complex, non-traditional design may require a reduction in the number of households using each access point, the removal of walkways connecting the blocks, restricting access by means of control access technology and concierges, the closure of unsafe areas such as underground garages and, less frequently, the complete remodelling of some 1960s and 1970s blocks and estates to create something which approximates traditional streetscapes. The aim of these improvements is to improve natural surveillance, confine access to residents and to create 'defensible space' around individual houses and blocks so that unwelcome non-residents are deterred from entering.[130] A number of these estates have been completely demolished and replaced with more traditional housing.

The notion that design improvements can reduce crime is a credible hypothesis and there is some evidence to support it.[131] However, design, although significant, is not usually the most important factor associated with high crime rates. There are many estates composed of conventionally designed houses and streetscapes which have high crime rates and many medium and high rise estates which have low rates. Much, of course, depends on who lives in the estates and how they are managed.

Research shows that it is 'child density' and the socioeconomic status of residents which have a greater influence on crime rates than design factors.[132] Crime rates are higher when there are concentrations of disadvantaged households and a high proportion of children relative to adults. To some extent, this can be prevented by housing management. Housing managers can, in some cases, ensure that there is a match between the design of estates, the types of household which are allocated accommodation on them and the style of management.

For example, communal housing in blocks of flats demands a more intensive style of management than estates of houses. Multi-storey blocks are not usually suitable for families with children but can be perfectly satisfactory accommodation for child-free households. While design alone does not 'cause' crime or affect it in a simple way, good design makes it easier for parents to supervise their children. It also makes estates more popular and easier to manage.

Neighbourhood management

Good neighbourhood management should help prevent both crime and what have been termed 'neighbourhood disorders' or incivilities such as drunkenness, hooliganism, harassment, disorderly and threatening behaviours, abandoned cars, flytipping, vandalism, anti-social behaviour and graffiti. In many areas, these are more of a problem than 'real crime' because they are much more commonplace and visible. If left unchecked, according to one plausible account, they generate fear and create the sort of disorderly, uncared for environment which attracts offenders, causes individuals and businesses to leave and results in neighbourhoods sliding into a spiral of decline from which it can be very difficult to recover.[133]

For the purposes of this chapter, three aspects of neighbourhood management will be discussed: housing services, preventive policing and community involvement.

Housing services. Neighbourhoods, particularly those characterised by a high proportion of social housing, are dependent for their viability on housing management and a range of related services such as maintenance, repairs, allocations, cleansing, caretaking and refuse collection. The quality of life in these areas can be improved substantially if such services are delivered effectively and responsively. During the 1980s, services in many areas were decentralised to improve responsiveness. While not always successful, decentralisation tried to ensure that gaps in provision were filled, duplication avoided and problems solved.

During the 1990s, there is some evidence that re-centralisation has occurred. This is partially in response to the demands of Compulsory Competitive Tendering which seems to be leading to larger, more centralised management teams instead of the small locally-based teams advocated in almost every report on the subject since the early 1980s.[134]

Quality housing management is vital, particularly at a time when pressure from ever increasing numbers of homeless households have led in some areas to concentrations of low income and disadvantaged households within the least desirable housing stock. The localised management style pioneered by the Priority Estates Project in partnership with social landlords emphasises tenant involvement, local control over budgets, service and allocations, and the deployment of caretakers, community wardens and concierges in order to create well managed and ordered environments.[135] A necessary precondition for reducing offence and offender rates on housing estates is responsive, local housing management.

It is the responsibility of social landlords to ensure that, wherever possible, estate design is matched with household type and that the number of children is not allowed to rise above a certain threshold. High child densities are invariably associated with vandalism and the problem is intensified if large numbers of children are housed within multi-storey blocks. Unfortunately, social landlords in some cities have no alternative but to house families in such blocks because 'right to buy' legislation has diminished their stock of houses and they are unable to build new houses in sufficient numbers to replace them. Their limited control over allocations can lead to concentrations of households with difficulties in inappropriately designed housing, a problem which can threaten the success of regeneration pro-grammes.[136]

However, even in these circumstances, preventive measures intro-duced by housing managers can be successful, particularly in combi-nation with those introduced by other agencies.[137] Aspects of housing management which can impact on crime and incivilities include effi-ciently managed resident caretakers and concierges; pro-active housing management from a local office; responsive repairs and preventive maintenance; enforcement of tenancy agreements; action to tackle neighbour disputes through mediation schemes; joint action by police and housing departments to tackle racial harassment and neighbour intimidation; setting up community warden patrols; and ensuring tenants with special needs receive appropriate care. Some local authorities which house their homeless families in tower blocks have allocated space for child care and pre-school provision.

Wherever possible, social landlords should consider deploying estate patrols as a means of compensating for the withdrawal of caretakers and regular police patrols in residential areas. For example, Swansea Council has taken this idea forward with great success.[138] It is an obvious way to supervise public areas and reduce the level of incivili-ties and anti-social behaviour that so often characterise them. They would undoubtedly be popular with residents. This idea could be developed in town and city centres, parks and other public spaces. In the Netherlands, where a similar approach has been adopted, surveys have shown an increase in public well-being (see chapter five).

Housing management was an important aspect of the regeneration of the 21 estates monitored by the Priority Estates Project and described in the publication *Swimming against the tide*.[139] In Meadowell and Scotswood in Newcastle, housing services set up inter-agency groups after the disturbances in 1991 and developed a model of responsive, local services. Problem solving housing management was a feature of work on the Halton Moor estate in Leeds where the housing managers, the estate management board and the police worked closely to address crime problems.

Investing in physical improvements to estates alone without attending to their subsequent management and maintenance is likely to result in the improvements being short lived. Good, localised housing management, particularly in combination with other preventive measures, can prevent problems occurring in the first place and prevent those that do occur from escalating.

Preventive policing. In chapter two ('Demolishing myths') it was argued that too much was expected of the criminal justice system as a means of preventing crime. However, the police obviously have a critical role to play – with others – in tackling crime problems in high crime neighbourhoods. Three policing strategies are particularly important: police enforcement, support for civil actions and problem solving approaches.[140]

Police enforcement includes targeting key offenders, carrying out high profile patrols and countering witness intimidation. In places with high levels of crime and disorder, an enforcement approach is often necessary to target known offenders and stabilise volatile situations. Obviously, this has to be managed carefully, particularly in areas where police-community relations are poor.

The police can also support civil actions taken by local authority housing enforcement teams to obtain injunctions against, or evictions of, persistently anti-social or criminal tenants. This was done on the

Kingsmead estate in Hackney and it led to substantial reduction in burglary and intimidation.[141]

Problem solving policing involves assigning officers to permanent neighbourhood beats and applying a 'problem solving approach' to address the root causes of crime and disorder problems. This involves identifying problems through crime pattern analysis, identifying the causes of these problems and devising preventive actions to address them. A close working relationship with other agencies and the community itself is essential. This approach requires officers to work in areas for two to three years to ensure consistency of policing style as well as personnel. This is crucial if relationships are to be built up and preventive projects given time to work.

This is not a call for the resurrection of a style of policing long since gone. Nor is this section advocating more 'traditional home beat policing' which in many areas commands low priority from police officers and is seen as unplanned, undirected and not very effective by local residents. Rather, it is arguing for the widespread replication of a much more sophisticated approach which is at the cutting edge of policing in some cities in the United States and some parts of the UK. It would mean that the police would be able to make an increased contribution to creating a safe and orderly neighbourhood instead of reacting to crime after the event. This approach has been endorsed by the Audit Commission in its 1996 report on street patrols.[142]

Problem solving policing was a key feature of the successful strategy to tackle the very high crime rate on the Pepys estate in south east London during the 1980s.[143] It was also applied on the Meadowell estate in Newcastle after the disturbances in the early 1990s, in Killingbeck, West Yorkshire, in Milton Keynes and in Toxteth, Merseyside.[144]

Pro-active policing is especially important when tackling crimes such as racial harassment, much of which involves crime against a person rather than against property. Unfortunately, this is not an area where there are many successful projects to showcase. In fact, one author has described the official response to this racial harassment as 'a vicious circle of inaction'.[145] There are often problems with implementing initiatives because agencies do not know what to do, there is a lack of commitment to act and community support is not always forthcoming.

However, successes have been achieved. In one project estate in east London, 67 per cent of Bengali families had been victimised repeatedly and had suffered 136 crimes over a six month period. Support for victims was provided and action taken against perpetrators (most of whom were neighbours). As a result, the proportion of families victimised dropped by 80 per cent. The key was decisive action by both the police and the local authority.[146]

Problem solving housing management and preventive policing can help create an orderly environment which will support the efforts of families to supervise their children. It is most likely to be successful if supported by the local community, which of course has its own important role to play in reducing youth crime and creating safer neighbourhoods. It is to this subject that we now turn.

Community involvement. In chapter three, it was argued that too much could be expected of local communities to prevent crime. Here, I want to consider the role they might realistically play. It is self-evident that local residents have an important role to play in enhancing the quality of life in their neighbourhoods and supporting each other in supervising their children. They can contribute to the management of schools in their role as school governors. They can set up playgroups and play and youth activities where they may serve as volunteers and on management committees. They have a contribution to make in planning design changes to their estates and may be involved to a greater or lesser degree in their management.

They may provide services through residents' associations, community mediation schemes, play and youth projects, and neighbourhood watches. In some areas, they have created development trusts which provide a raft of community services. There is an increasing bank of knowledge on good practice and on what form of involvement is most sustainable. It is almost certainly the case that much of the social and recreational provision considered desirable in neighbourhoods is not viable without a significant input of local volunteer labour.

However, there are two preconditions for maximising the voluntary involvement of local residents. The first is an effective response by the key statutory agencies to the problems that only they have the authority and resources to tackle. The most important of these agencies are the police and the local authority. This is not always recognised and a feature of community crime prevention is an over-dependence on voluntary effort. In such circumstances, those who do become involved rapidly become despondent when faced with apparently insoluble problems. On the Kingsmead estate mentioned earlier, a very successful community trust was able to establish itself once the housing department and police had dealt with the most serious problems.[147]

The second is an adequate system for recruiting and supporting volunteers. Volunteers need not only come from the immediate locality and a system has to be in place for recruiting, assessing, training and placing them. Local young people should be encouraged to participate as volunteer youth and community workers. Many will be very good at it and may take it up as a career. This has been a feature of the Youthworks project in Blackburn.

Emphasis should also be placed on involving unemployed people. Skills audits can identify a wide range of local commitment and expertise that might otherwise go unused. Just as too much can be left to voluntary effort, agencies cannot solve neighbourhood problems unless there is a significant degree of community involvement. Multi-agency work at a neighbourhood level should create the context in which local voluntary effort is most likely to flourish.

For this to happen, additional support is often needed. The Department of Health's Opportunities for Volunteering Fund (now in its tenth year) is an excellent source of such support. It supports voluntary activity in a large number of disadvantaged areas by providing grants for full-time volunteer organisers and resources for equipment and transport. Grants from funds such as this lever many times their value in terms of volunteer labour and additional resources generated by fundraising efforts. Much of this voluntary activity provides facilities for families, children and young people. In doing so, it strengthens communities and makes a significant contribution to supervising the young, providing them with recreational, social and educational opportunities and diverting them from offending.[148]

Summary: safer neighbourhoods
This section has discussed how improved security and design on the one hand and neighbourhood services and policing on the other can

reduce crime and disorder and enhance community safety. The concept of neighbourhood management has been introduced and the importance of preventive, pro-active services emphasised. The crucial role that the community itself can play has been stressed.

The comprehensive approach to prevention advocated here draws on evaluated practice from this country and abroad and – more often – from promising initiatives which have not been rigorously evaluated but which appear from careful monitoring to be effective. Its aim is to reduce crime and disorder problems now and to put in place measures which will reduce their incidence in the future. Particular consideration should be given to combining improvements in the way neighbourhoods are designed and serviced with support for families and initiatives focused on education, youth and employment. If this is to be achieved, effective and coordinated multi-agency action at a neighbourhood level is required. This is not always easy to bring about. First, much of what needs to be done to prevent crime and criminality is not a truly core concern of any of the agencies involved. Second, it is difficult for any one agency to exercise leadership over a multi-agency initiative. We will now suggest ways of overcoming this problem.

4. Developing a local strategy

Most discussion about preventing crime concerns *what* should be done. Much less attention has been paid to *how* it should be done. This is unfortunate. Well planned initiatives will always fail if they are not implemented properly and, as will be seen, this is very common. This chapter will therefore focus on how to implement local strategies successfully. Particular attention will be paid to management and leadership.

Making partnerships work

Since 1984, government has promoted multi-agency partnerships (involving the police, local authority, probation service and private sector) as the primary mechanism for planning and implementing crime prevention activity.[149] There are now about 250 partnerships in England and Wales. Soon there will be one for every local authority. It is timely to ask the question: how effective are they?

At their best, they are able to mobilise agencies, coordinate effort, focus resources and reduce crime. They can tackle problems which would be well beyond the reach of agencies acting alone. However, many partnerships have found it rather difficult to deliver effective crime prevention. This is partly because preventing crime is difficult: we do not know how much there is; there is no agreement about how to prevent it; crime prevention is not the responsibility of any one agency; local efforts are constrained by national policies; there are few extra resources; coordinating the input of agencies in high crime areas can be difficult to organise.

There are also other reasons why partnerships do not always achieve what is expected of them. First, the partnership is seen as an end in itself rather than a means to an end. Second, there is confusion about the role of the multi-agency group on the one hand and the individual agencies on the other. Third, partnerships fail to implement a focused programme of work. Fourth, they do not address the whole problem. Finally, they fail to achieve durability. Let us look at these in turn.

A means to an end?

Partnerships, steering groups and multi-agency committees do not prevent crime. They talk about preventing crime. If they are to prevent crime, certain conditions have to be present. They have to be well chaired, fully supported by key agencies at a senior level – especially the police and local authority – and highly focused. Strong leadership and close liaison between the police and senior officers and members of the local authority are particularly important. There should be one strategic partnership for each town or city although local multi-agency groups may be set up to tackle problems in particular localities.

Research suggests that these conditions are not really negotiable. If they are met, partnerships are more likely to succeed. If they are not, there is the danger that they will generate a lot of paper and talk but little else. Partnerships are a means to an end, not an end in themselves.

Multi-agency planning, single agency action

If multi-agency partnerships are to be effective, the individual agencies that compose them have to develop their own crime prevention capacity. This is an absolutely crucial point that is not always fully understood. Of these agencies, the most important one is the local authority. This can be achieved through an 'in-house' community safety strategy which enables the authority to:

- prevent crime against its employees, property, equipment and those for whom it is responsible
- prevent criminality through the work of social services, education and the youth service
- contribute to multi-agency prevention work.

All services should be required to identify in their annual plans how they will contribute to corporate crime prevention and community safety objectives. In Kirklees, for example, this has been done in the following way:

Community safety subcommittee
(members; officers; police; probation)
To decide policy, review progress

Interdepartmental officer group
(second or third tier)
To implement policy

Task groups
To work with individual services
To put in place risk management procedures
To develop action in specific localities.

This is not the only way to do it. But it has a number of advantages. It makes sure that there is coordination between elected members and officers. It builds community safety and crime prevention into main-stream services so added value is obtained from existing expenditure. Finally, it helps the authority to play its part in making the multi-agency partnership successful.

To illustrate the importance of this point, let us consider an example. A multi-agency initiative to tackle crime problems on a housing estate may not succeed or will take much longer to work if the housing department does not deliver its mainstream services in a way that is conducive to crime prevention and safety, if the police have not developed models of effective community policing and if outreach youth work is not promoted by the youth service. The problems will be endlessly discussed and rarely resolved.

Multi-agency partnerships will therefore be more effective when the preventive capacity of single agencies and departments has been developed.[150] I have given the example of the local authority but the same principle applies to the police and other agencies. If this is not done, agencies and departments pass their crime prevention responsibility on to the multi-agency group whose agenda then becomes overloaded. It also means that the actions that need to be taken by individual agencies to make the multi-agency group succeed may not be taken.

A focused programme of work

The third problem experienced by partnerships is their failure to develop a focused programme of work. Often, they are not sure what, if anything, they have achieved. Did they have clear objectives? Were the projects they set up well managed? Were they evaluated? They may be confident with regard to home security schemes for example. But what about youth projects or measures to tackle domestic violence or racial harassment? Are they effective? Did they reduce the problem they were set up to tackle?

Too often, crime prevention and community safety work is insufficiently rigorous. We do not always assess or prioritise problems carefully. We often decide what we are going to do about them without considering a range of options. We frequently pay too little attention to implementation. We try to do much with too little and achieve nothing because the dosage of our interventions is too weak. We rarely monitor progress or evaluate outcomes. As a result, we have no idea at all whether what we have done has worked or not, although we usually say it has.

It is easy to be too negative – there are many examples of first rate work all over the country. But these are common pitfalls which are best anticipated. We need to apply the same high standards of management to crime prevention and community safety as are increasingly demanded for other public services. The work must be outcome focused; it must be seen to make a difference. How?

There are two ways of making sure of success. First, a problem solving, systematic approach should be adopted. This involves an agreed vision of what is to be achieved, strong leadership, commitment, continuity of key staff and application of the methodology as follows:[151]

1. Secure support of key players
2. Assess problems accurately
3. Agree priorities and set up task groups

4. Decide what to do carefully
5. Prepare detailed action plan
6. Assign responsibility for implementation
7. Monitor progress and evaluate impact.

Secure support. It is essential to secure the active support of agency leaders, establish and train a steering committee and agree a framework for action. It is worth investing time in making sure that all involved are agreed on the overall approach and are committed, at least in principle, to take action. It is important to secure the services of an effective chair and this can be helpful to organise a team building and induction event.

Assess problems. Crime problems can be assessed by undertaking or commissioning a crime audit. This involves collecting and interpreting recorded crime statistics, carrying out surveys, consulting residents and agencies, presenting findings and deciding priorities. Audits provide objective information to help decide priorities and baseline data to allow evaluation to be undertaken. Where time is short, rapid appraisals can be undertaken. These take much less time (three to five days) than a full audit but can only be undertaken by experienced staff.

Agree priorities and set up task groups. It is unlikely that a partnership will be able to tackle all the problems in an area at the same time. They will need to select those which deserve the most urgent attention. The number identified will depend on the level of resources available to make a difference. Task groups can be set up to progress work in particular localities.

Decide what to do. Having agreed priorities, it is necessary to decide how to respond to them. This involves selecting, testing, comparing and agreeing options (option appraisal). This aims to clarify the outcome sought, the mechanism by which each option is likely to bring about the outcome and the conditions that have to be present for it to work.[152] This process is often overlooked. As a result, inappropriate measures may be implemented which do not work. It is best to select options that are based on tried and tested approaches.

Prepare action plan. This involves preparing a detailed plan which states what is going to be done by whom, by when and with what results. It should be precise and achievable. It is at this point that service agreements should be obtained with agencies that have agreed to deliver parts of the plan.

Assign responsibility for implementation. Implementation failure is common and its causes numerous. One researcher has identified fourteen reasons for it:[153]

- Shortage of resources
- Too small or large catchment area
- Unrealistic objectives
- Lack of focus
- Programme drift
- Inappropriate targets
- Low client attendance and attrition
- Lack of support for volunteers
- Poor programme design
- Lack of monitoring
- Inadequacy of physical facilities
- Inadequate staffing levels
- Poor information and recordkeeping
- Technology failure.

Implementation failure can be avoided by assigning authority and responsibility to a lead officer, ensuring that objectives and performance indicators are drawn up and that there is a clear understanding of what is to be undertaken by whom. The importance of strong, focused management cannot be overstated.

Monitor progress and evaluate impact. Monitoring ensures that progress is reviewed at regular intervals and adjustments are made if necessary to ensure the project achieves its objectives. This is simply good management. Evaluation, on the other hand, is concerned with answering six questions:

- *Process.* Was the programme implemented as planned?
- *Impact.* Did it make a difference to priority problems?
- *Cost-benefit.* Were the benefits greater than the costs?
- *Credibility.* Was the programme credible with the community?
- *Durability.* Did the benefits last?
- *Replicability.* Can it be developed in other areas?

This work is usually undertaken by someone with specialist evaluation skills.

This approach to managing crime prevention and community safety initiatives is similar to that advocated by criminologists over recent years in order to encourage a more rational and analytical approach to crime management. In reality, the process of developing crime prevention initiatives is less linear and more complicated. Political factors may override 'rational' decisions (sometimes for good reasons). Opportunities unrelated to need may appear which are too good to ignore and new directions will be taken as a result of changes in membership. Priorities may change over time.

Nevertheless, it is valuable for groups to develop a clear set of objectives and set a course to achieve them, even if they choose a different route along the way. Recognising the need for a more planned, problem solving approach to prevention is necessary if the field is to move forward from an uninformed, 'do what feels best' approach.

The second way of ensuring success is to do enough to make a difference. For any crime to occur, three conditions must be present: the opportunity, a willing offender and the absence of a capable guardian. The most effective and enduring crime prevention projects, therefore, are often those which address more than one of these elements. So to prevent burglary, it may be necessary to reduce opportunities by improving the security of vulnerable homes, to reduce the number of willing offenders by targeting persistent offenders, and to increase the number of capable guardians through police patrols, Neighbourhood Watch or CCTV.

It is also important to make sure that the dosage of each intervention is sufficient. If a doctor treating a patient gives them only half the vaccine that is needed, the patient will not be adequately protected. The same principle applies to crime prevention. In the case of the burglary example, has enough been done to secure the homes adequately? Have enough homes been secured to bring down the neighbourhood burglary rate? Has enough been done to target persistent offenders and divert those young people who may be at risk of becoming frequent offenders? Are there enough capable guardians to deter and prevent burglary? Community safety strategies should therefore follow three key principles:

- They focus on a limited number of geographical areas; they do not try to spread themselves too thinly.
- In these targeted areas, they put in place a customised package of carefully selected measures. Single measures are usually not enough; often a crime problem has to be tackled from two or more angles and there is usually more than one crime problem to address.
- They pay obsessive attention to project design, implementation and evaluation.

Tackling the whole problem
In chapter three, a thematic approach to preventing crime and criminality at a neighbourhood level was presented in detail and the importance of addressing the whole problem was stressed. The goal is to reduce risk factors and enhance protective factors at different developmental stages (early childhood, primary school years, adolescence and early adulthood), to make crime more difficult to commit and to deal effectively with those who do offend. Not everything can be done and what is prioritised locally will depend on the outcome of a risk and crime audit. However, partnerships which rely on only one preventive measure will only be addressing part of the problem and it may not be enough to make an impact.

Durability
Most will agree that community safety strategies should not only be concerned with special projects to deal with particular problems. There are two other important objectives. The first is to make prevention part of the routine day-to-day practice and culture of all agencies and individuals to avoid at least some of the problems occurring in the first place. The second is to develop longer-term multi-agency strategies that can impact on the most serious problems. While programmes and projects are worthwhile in their own right, they are doubly valuable if they can lead the way to these more permanent arrangements. There are four key elements of a durable, multi-agency strategy:[154]

- *Acceptance of responsibility by individual agencies,* by incorporating community safety objectives within their mainstream services.

Developing a local strategy

Form partnership Define problems (Crime audit, surveys, consultations) Agree priorities and set up task groups

↓

Appraise options Prepare action plan (Objectives, service agreements, performance indicators) Assign responsibility

↓

Implement action: Early childhood prevention Opportunities for young people Safer neighbourhoods

↓

Mainstream services Monitor progress

↓

Evaluate impact: process outcomes costs/benefits credibility durability replicability

- *Cooperation between agencies,* both formally through strategic multi-agency groups, and informally in the neighbourhoods and on the streets.
- *A shared strategy,* that is, an agreed approach to tackling priority problems.
- *Agency policies that reflect the shared strategy.* This is vital to ensure that individual agencies are able to contribute to implementing the shared strategy. It is also necessary to ensure that available resources are properly coordinated and targeted.

The goal here is to mainstream community safety so that it becomes a core part of local governance. Achieving a durable strategy is not easy and will require persistence, leadership and support from the top.

Summary

This chapter has suggested how crime and criminality prevention can be reduced by sustained, planned and coordinated action. Particular emphasis has been paid to the mechanisms by which prevention works. This is crucial. For example, it is quite possible for pre-school or youth work provision – two of the approaches advocated in the previous chapter – to have no preventive benefit at all. Whether they do or not depends on how they are planned, targeted and managed. Measures to prevent crime and criminality will only work if these preventive mechanisms are made explicit and inform the planning of all preventive activity.

The knowledge and experience that underpin this book draw on a relatively small number of pilot projects and are not systematically applied to routine prevention work. It is now time to incorporate good preventive practice within mainstream services so that crime reductions can be achieved more widely and then sustained. This requires a national crime prevention strategy which clarifies the role of all the key players nationally and locally, sets targets and provides the means by which they will be achieved. This is the subject of the next chapter.

5. Towards prevention: national policy, local governance

Throughout this book, I have argued that criminal justice policy needs to make a decisive shift giving greater emphasis to prevention. Before considering how central government and local agencies might do this, it is worth considering the rapid social change that has occurred in the post-war period and the policies that have been developed in response, particularly those concerned with urban regeneration during the 1990s. It will help explain why a change in the way crime and disorder problems are managed is so necessary.

By the 1960s, the widespread, though qualified, support for law and order that characterised the period from 1890 to 1950 had begun to unravel. American theories linking crime with social disorganisation and economic disadvantage seemed to have more validity in the UK than before.[155] Society had become more heterogeneous and complex, there was a decline in respect for all kinds of authority and a demand for individual freedom of expression was made possible by increased prosperity and a liberalisation of attitudes.

At the same time, post-war urban development and changes in the labour and housing markets led to a dramatic change in the nature of urban communities. There was a decline in community cohesion and associated informal community controls. These developments in turn led to an increase in crime and other indicators of social disorder. In some areas, this was exacerbated by the economic changes which took place during the 1980s and 1990s and which resulted in a significant loss in semi-skilled and unskilled work. Unemployment among young people – especially young men – became a major political issue. These tensions, sometimes intensified by poor relations with the police, led to several episodes of urban disturbances. Neither government, the criminal justice agencies nor the apparatus of local governance seemed able to manage this situation confidently.

This is not surprising. For some, these agencies were characterised by a bureaucratic, reactive ethos that was not capable of adapting to rapidly changing circumstances. Indeed, it is often argued that they were concerned mainly with administering rather than resolving problems and managing the process of national decline in an orderly manner. It gradually became clear that urban governance needed to become much more problem solving, pro-active and concerned with regeneration.

In the 1970s and 1980s, there were numerous experiments led by central or local government, specialist agencies and various kinds of partnerships. By 1994, twenty separate government programmes had been integrated within a Single Regeneration Budget (SRB). This was a major attempt to ensure that regeneration was comprehensive, geared to local needs, targeted in small areas (with populations of approximately 25,000), delivered by multi-agency partnerships, output focused and durable.

Unfortunately, developments in the prevention of crime have not, by and large, kept up with those in regeneration policy. In 1984, government recognised that the police could not prevent crime on their own and that the resources of other agencies needed to be mobilised in the form of multi-agency partnerships to help them.[156] In addition, there were a large number of pilot programmes and research studies. But the mechanisms were never clearly thought through. The emphasis given to the partnership approach represents a crucial stepping stone between old and new ways of controlling crime.

A national strategy

There is now growing recognition of the need for a national crime prevention and community safety strategy that draws on the substantial experience and research of the past ten years and aims to achieve specific crime reduction targets. Overseen by a crime prevention agency or directorate within the Home Office, this might involve:

- coordinating the contribution of government departments and ensuring more efficient, interdepartmental work
- providing guidance on legislation, policy and resources
- setting standards, recommending crime prevention regulations, promoting training and professional certification, commissioning research
- devising incentives for public and private sector institutions to invest in prevention
- reviewing ways of adjusting the balance of expenditure between prevention and the criminal justice system
- considering how the criminal justice agencies could have more of a preventive impact
- requiring contracts or partnerships with local authorities to prepare and deliver crime prevention and community safety plans
- securing resources for local strategies
- ensuring that sufficient technical assistance is available to support local partnerships
- ensuring that successful practice is mainstreamed.

The brief should be broad enough to include crime prevention, criminality prevention and community safety activity. It should introduce some order, coherence and standards into a subject area that is seriously underprofessionalised. It should have a budget so that it is better able to support local crime prevention initiatives, perhaps on a matched funding basis. It should have a limited number of priority themes which might include high crime neighbourhoods, youth crime, crime against women and crime in the workplace. Emphasis should be placed on setting and achieving clear crime prevention targets. This work has already started. Wide representation on a national crime prevention council, most particularly the inclusion of local government representatives, would increase its status and influence. Such a strategy would create the conditions for successful crime prevention at a local level.

Local governance
There are various views about which agency should be responsible for the delivery of community safety at a local level and how this might

be done. The 1993 Morgan report on the local delivery of crime prevention recommended that responsibility should be assigned to local authorities and this is currently the policy of the new Local Government Association.[157]

Some senior police figures feel that responsibility should not be passed to local authorities because many elements of the problem fall outside of local authority jurisdiction (for example, vehicle crime, retail crime, application of preventive technology, liaison with manufacturers). Moreover, it is argued that the role of local authorities in local governance has diminished in the years since the publication of the Morgan report. Some feel that since police authorities have statutory responsibilities to publish plans which must involve community safety, responsibility should be passed to them.

The 1996 Police Foundation/Policy Studies report on the role and responsibilities of the police recommends that local authorities be required to prepare draft community safety plans for submission to the police authority for approval. It also suggests that the boundaries of police-community consultative groups (PCCGs) be changed so that their areas cover those of local authorities (as is the case in London) and that PCCGs be the vehicle of communication between the police authority and the local authority. It clearly assigns the lead role for crime prevention and community safety strategies to police authorities.[158]

This report is one of the very few to have reviewed this issue in detail. Its main drawback, however, is that it assumes that community safety is a branch of policing. In chapter two, the contribution and the limitations of the police to prevention were discussed. It concluded that most policing is not preventive and most community safety work is not undertaken by the police.

A statutory obligation should instead be placed on both police authority and local authorities (unitary and district councils) to prepare annual, costed, community safety plans in consultation with other relevant agencies (which would include county councils in areas with two tier local government). Parish councils might also be encouraged to prepare plans. Progress against the plans could be monitored in the same way as policing plans are monitored.

The police authority would be responsible for ensuring that the policing contribution to such plans was agreed and operationalised. They would also be responsible for ensuring that partnership approaches to prevention were promoted with local authorities where they did not already exist and for consulting with local authorities about policing strategies. In addition, policing authorities are well placed to stimulate more investment in prevention by allocating, say, 5 per cent of their budgets to resource safety plans.

Responsibility for negotiating and implementing an acceptable plan would be down to the local authority in partnership, of course, with the police and others. This is, in effect, what happens at present. It is doubtful that local authorities would, in any case, want to defer to the police authority on this matter. The local authority is the appropriate level of local governance for such a function and is (still) responsible directly or indirectly for a wide range of services which can have important community safety effects.

If local authorities were to be given a statutory responsibility for preparing an annual community safety plan, they might be encouraged to:

- assign a senior official to work to the chief executive or establish a community safety unit in the chief executive's department, as many have already done
- build crime prevention into the thinking of all departments by setting up an interdepartmental officers' group and requiring departments to identify and achieve departmental crime prevention objectives
- require local authority committees to consider the impact on crime of any decisions they may take
- establish a high level multi-agency partnership group
- carry out a crime audit, including assessment
- prepare a costed, annual community safety plan which addresses:
  - high crime neighbourhoods
  - crime by young people
  - crime in town or city centres
  - safer travel
  - domestic violence

(crime against women, ethnic minority groups and children should inform all themes)

- provide training for community safety staff, other staff with a community safety function and their managers
- ensure that crime and criminality prevention are incorporated within regeneration programmes
- monitor progress against real crime prevention targets.

The major question is how to fund an increase in crime prevention and community safety work. The principles underpinning the SRB challenge fund, currently the main source of funding for crime prevention and community safety work, mean that resources cannot be earmarked specifically for crime prevention and community safety. Furthermore, a selective challenge fund cannot, by definition, meet the widespread need for assistance. Government should consider increasing the Standard Spending Assessments of local authorities to take account of increased responsibilities or making grants on a matched funding basis. Alternatively, it could consider the example of the French 'Contrat de ville'. This involves a negotiation between central and local government over what central government will fund and what local government will deliver. It is needs based and does not involve competition with others. This is similar to the approach taken by the Netherlands discussed at the end of this chapter (see page 105).

Mainstreaming services

The greatest opportunity, however, for reducing crime and enhancing safety is through incorporating preventive objectives within mainstream services and delivering these services much more pro-actively than is commonly the case. The most important services in this regard are policing, housing management, social services, education, the youth service and health.

Policing

Preventive, problem solving policing by dedicated police officers can make a significant difference to the speed with which crime and disorder problems are resolved. This is particularly so when they work closely with housing managers and others. As was noted in the last chapter, 80 per cent of the perpetrators of racial harassment on one estate desisted when visited by police and housing managers who made it clear that further offending would lead to eviction. The police are also key players in ensuring that prevention is concentrated on those who have been victims and linking the prevention of repeat victimisation to the detection of frequent offenders.

Housing management

The key to preventive management is encouraging managers to become pro-active problem solvers. This involves conducting regular visits and audits, identifying minor problems before they become serious, helping create a sense of order and developing relationships with police officers, youth workers, tenants' leaders and so on. This is a broader role than simply carrying out the limited housing management functions that may be specified in contracts awarded under Compulsory Competitive Tendering. It involves staff becoming problem solving managers rather than administrators. In Coventry, a similar approach has been encouraged by assigning responsibility for preparing and implementing inter-agency plans to coordinators with responsibility for defined geographical areas.[159]

Social services

Social services departments have principal responsibility for the welfare of children and young people and it is to them that local authorities turn to carry out the duty 'to take action to reduce delinquency' in the Children Act. Most have prepared Children's Plans but most of their resources continue to be devoted to responding to child abuse and monitoring children and families on the Child Protection Register.[160] Furthermore, the quality of much preventive work is very variable and outcomes rarely known. An Audit Commission report recommended that social services departments give greater emphasis to prevention but failed to indicate whether this should be done at the cost of reducing its vigilance on child abuse.[161]

Education

The role of the education service in helping schools reduce truancy, school failure and exclusion and ensuring that excluded pupils are returned to full-time education and training was discussed in detail in chapter three. The contribution of schools and local education authorities to preventing criminality needs to be acknowledged explicitly. Additional support for schools will be necessary if this contribution is to increased.

Youth service

The youth service can help reduce problems of youth crime and anti-social behaviour on estates by targeting their resources in disadvantaged neighbourhoods, using outreach or detached workers and working with those young people who are most at risk. There has, in the past, been some resistance by youth workers to adopting this role. The youth service needs to be rebuilt with the prevention of offending and anti-social behaviour by young people as one of its main objectives.

Health

Health authorities are responsible for primary health care, school nurses, drug and health education, and mental health services. Health professionals in primary health care teams (especially health visitors and midwives) are able to identify families and communities at risk and are often an important source of parenting advice.

Unfortunately, the special projects in which preventive practice is tested are usually short-term, one-off pilot initiatives. The differences in style and content to regular services (which were responsible for their success) do not, surprisingly, often seem to inform mainstream service delivery. It is beyond the scope of this book to account for this failure. It is less a question of resources and more one of bureaucratic inertia, poor management and, occasionally, professional resistance.

'Mainstreaming' crime prevention and community safety has major implications for public sector management and the professional training of police officers, housing officers, youth workers, social workers, probation officers and others. Relentless budget cuts and the tendency of central government to marginalise local government has contributed to a crisis of purpose among those working in the public sector. As a result, many staff are suffering from poor morale. What is needed is a performance-oriented, management culture that is able to motivate staff to deliver consistently high quality services. It will be hard to argue for more resources when best use is not being made of those we already have.

Incorporating more preventive practice into mainstream service delivery – creating a culture of prevention – is the key to sustaining reductions in crime and extending the scope of preventive activity. Demonstrating convincingly that these services can prevent crime and disorder is necessary if additional resources are to be secured. Showing that they can be cost effective is the best way of generating long-term support and investment.

Costs, resources and benefits

Those who argue that the measures necessary to prevent crime will cost a lot of money should be reminded that crime is already costing a lot of money. There are the direct financial losses incurred as a result of fraud, property theft or damage. There are the social costs incurred through personal crime and violence. There are the consequential costs generated by all offences, including the costs of inconvenience, disruption, investigation, services to victims and loss of business. There are the costs of the criminal justice agencies. Furthermore, there can be substantial economic costs if crime causes neighbourhoods to deteriorate. These costs are measured in billions of pounds.

Audit after audit in the UK has confirmed the high and unacceptable costs of crime to government, the private sector and the individual. There have been many attempts to quantify them but few have assessed the financial and other benefits of prevention. Would increased investment in prevention – the approach advocated in this book – be good value for money? Do the benefits of spending more on prevention outweigh the costs? Is it worth doing?

Estimating the financial benefits of prevention is difficult. The methodology is complicated. There are considerable data collection problems to be overcome and it is not easy to quantify non-monetary costs and benefits. While it is true that direct losses can be reduced through preventive action (sometimes by redeploying existing resources), the costs of prevention will sometimes exceed reductions in direct losses that they bring about. It is only when all the quantifiable non-monetary and unquantifiable costs and benefits are taken into account that a fair judgement can be made. In fact, it is these latter kinds of benefits (such as reduced fear of crime, improved quality of life, reduced demands on services) that are likely to be the key to final decisions about the balance of costs and benefits.[162]

Relatively little attention has been paid to cost-benefit analysis in the crime prevention and community safety field although it is routinely applied to other social policy areas such as housing investment. Drawing on the themes adopted for chapter three, let us consider some examples of where it has been attempted.

Early childhood prevention

Evaluators of the American Perry Pre-school Project quoted in chapter three estimated that for every dollar invested in high quality pre-school education for disadvantaged children, $7 were saved over the next twenty plus years through less crime, drug misuse, welfare dependency and unemployment. Similar figures have been cited for other US prevention programmes. There is no reason to suppose that quality preventive services – family support, pre-school and parenting programmes – would not be a good investment in the UK, returning real and measurable short-term and long-term benefits. One recent set of American calculations suggest that parenting education could be one of the most cost effective means of reducing reducing later serious crime.

A 1996 study by the Rand Corporation in the United States compared the cost effectiveness of early intervention programmes with repeat offender, minimum sentence imprisonment. It found that three of the four early intervention approaches compared favourably in cost effectiveness with imprisonment, as measured by the number of serious crimes prevented for every $1 million spent on the programme. It considered that more large scale demonstration programmes are necessary to test this provisional finding and assess the input of different approaches on crime rates.[163] More work is needed to quantify the costs and benefits of early childhood prevention in the UK.

Opportunities for young people

According to research undertaken by the accountants Coopers & Lybrand for the Prince's Trust, youth crime prevention projects do not have to prevent many crimes before they start to cover their costs. This research estimated the cost of each youth crime at £2,300. If prevented, 50 per cent would be recoverable. Based on a sample of projects, it was estimated that they would need to prevent an offence by a ratio of 1:5 to 1:14 of participants or reduce the total offending record of each participant by one offence. Many projects will be much more effective than this. These findings are encouraging and confirm what many have felt for some time.[164]

However, the research was very clear about the types of youth project that would have this preventive effect. They had to be targeted in areas with a high proportion of young people offending or at risk of offending, have clear objectives, be intensive, educational and challenging and be reasonably long term.

Safer neighbourhoods
A cost-benefit analysis of Crime Concern's Homesafe Burglary Prevention projects located in seven Safer Cities sites estimated that the cost of a single burglary to the victims after insurance recovery was £1,100 and that targeting victims would be a cost effective way of reducing the overall neighbourhood burglary rate. In Blackburn, for example, the cost of making 307 properties in one neighbourhood secure was £41,000. There were 58 less burglaries in the Homesafe year compared to the previous year so the saving was £64,000 (58 x £1,100), producing a net gain of £23,000. When compared with control areas, the Blackburn target area avoided a sharp increase which took place during the Homesafe year so the reduction in burglary can be reasonably attributed to the project.[165]

The Homesafe evaluation estimated net savings of between £23,000 and £121,000 for four of the five sites studied in detail. In the fifth, there was a net loss because of the low initial crime rate in the area and problems with making multiply-occupied houses more secure. It concluded that the key to securing a favourable cost-benefit ratio is to select sites with at least a 6 per cent burglary rate and preferably higher, with between 1,500 and 3,000 properties, and to ensure at least 10 per cent are secured in one year.

These calculations did not include putative savings in the costs of the criminal justice agencies as some cost-benefit analyses have done.

However, it is worth noting that in Merthyr Tydfil, it was assessed that sixteen hours of police time were saved for every burglary prevented so there was a substantial opportunity benefit for the police. The Homesafe evaluation did take account of the effect of other interventions but most of these came on stream after Homesafe. It also took account of crime trends in the surrounding area.

In addition to the benefits of reduction in crime, there were also benefits in terms of reduced fear of crime, increased confidence, improved multi-agency working and increased willingness of residents to play a positive part in their community. Tackling domestic burglary, a crime which could potentially affect all residents, was a suitable springboard for the development of other initiatives in the areas.

Let us now consider how the costs and benefits of implementing the comprehensive approach advocated in this book might be assessed at a neighbourhood level. For example, a housing estate may have a high burglary rate and problems with anti-social behaviour by young people. As a result, it has become unpopular and its properties difficult to let. It is known that fifteen to nineteen year olds living on the estate are principally responsible. Simply target hardening the homes may displace the burglary to commercial premises or to another type of crime such as robbery. Following analysis of the problem and appraisal of various options, it is decided to take vigorous management action aimed at the most persistent offenders (including injunctions leading to eviction), put in place a burglary prevention project to prevent repeat victimisation and set up a youth work project with an outreach worker to divert young people from crime and expose them to more constructive activities.

The cost of these measures might be £80,000 (£30,000 for burglary prevention, £40,000 for the youth project, £10,000 for legal costs). An evaluation would assess the quantifiable monetary benefits in terms of savings for householders and landlord. Examples of these have already been demonstrated in connection with the Homesafe projects. Using benchmark figures, the monetary benefits of other crimes reduced (such as car crime or vandalism) could be assessed. In addition, other quantifiable monetary benefits might include reduced costs of repairs to the landlord, properties easier to let, lower staff sickness and turnover among agencies working in the area, less victimisation of local businesses, and, possibly, fewer school exclusions.

Quantifiable non-monetary benefits would include fewer demands on the police, social services, housing and other agencies, greater insurability, increased employer confidence in residents as potential employees and increased business activity. Unquantifiable benefits would include reduced fear of crime, improved quality of life and reduced stigma of neighbourhood.

It is important to assess all the costs and benefits to all interested parties: the agencies, businesses, residents and any others. In this example, it would be desirable to be able to show that at least £80,000 in benefits accrued to them as a result of these interventions. Successful projects in high crime areas would not find this difficult. When the benefits that are more difficult to quantify are included, it is probable that most well planned and managed prevention projects in high crime areas will be good value for money.

The work so far undertaken on the cost effectiveness of prevention is relatively unsophisticated. But it indicates possibilities that must be explored. More work is necessary to determine the most cost effective means of tackling particular crime problems, the benefits that are likely to follow and what financial mechanism is required to encourage more investment in prevention to be undertaken, given that the agencies which are often asked to make the investment (the local authorities) are often not those to whom the financial benefits accrue (the criminal justice system). Such work is essential if we are to be able to argue convincingly that investing £1 billion in prevention represents better value for money than, for example, spending it on new prisons. The financial benefits of prevention will really start to be felt when there is sufficient investment to reduce crime to a level at which direct savings in the costs of prisons, courts, and police can be made.

However, since some would argue that we should increase spending on the criminal justice agencies to reduce crime, it is worth considering the cost effectiveness of the two most common 'solutions' to the crime problem: greater use of imprisonment and more police officers.

Greater use of imprisonment will reduce crime but not by very much and at considerable cost. Home Office research estimated that an increase of 25 per cent in the size of the prison population would reduce the crime rate by only 1 per cent.[166] This would mean increasing prison numbers by over 12,000. Apart from any moral objections, it would be hard to justify such an increase (with all its attendant costs including a massive prison building programme) to achieve such a small reduction in crime.

Similarly, it has been calculated that a 1 per cent increase in police numbers would increase the clear up rate by a mere 0.15 per cent. To reduce property crime by 1 per cent by employing more police officers would cost £51 million.[167]

Given the poor value for money represented by these traditional responses to crime, investing more in prevention may be a sensible policy to pursue. How might it be funded?

Resources to invest in the programmes suggested in this book could come from a number of sources. The Audit Commission has shown how reductions can be made in the cost of processing young offenders (currently £1 billion). For example, if one in five young people accepted a caution plus programme instead of being processed through the courts, about £40 million per year could be released to fund preventive services. In addition, a cap should be placed on the use of imprisonment and cheaper, more effective alternatives used for non-violent offenders. This would, in time, free up resources for prevention.

It had already been suggested that police authorities could assign a proportion of their budget to prevention. Reduced offending will also be achieved by ensuring that preventive mechanisms inform the delivery of services met by non-criminal justice budgets, for example, those concerned with health, education, social services and housing and regeneration. Added preventive value would thereby be obtained from existing expenditure. The next government should aim to increase direct expenditure on prevention from 0.37 per cent to 1 per cent of the criminal justice budget and to 5 per cent over the lifetime of two parliaments. This might be made possible by setting up a system of borrowing against hypothecated projected future savings which would be internal to government, rather than making a net addition to the PSBR.

Investing £100,000 annually for five years in 1,000 high crime neighbourhoods (and their associated schools and business areas) would make a major impact on crime and criminality in these areas and elsewhere. It would cost £100 million per year, the cost of building three new secure training centres.[168] In addition, it would certainly stimulate better preventive use of existing mainstream resources and lever additional resources and effort from the wider community and private sector. It is probable that the quantifiable financial benefits alone would be considerably greater than the costs. From a Treasury perspective, it would represent very good value for money.

A view from the Netherlands

This book has drawn on American research findings to demonstrate that specific preventive approaches can work. Before concluding this chapter, it will look to Europe and consider the partnership between national and local government that has been developed in the Netherlands to implement a preventive strategy.

Major Cities Memorandum

In 1994, a report on juvenile crime advocated a multi-agency approach to juvenile crime, the main recommendations of which are now being implemented as part of the government's Major Cities Memorandum. This involves partnerships between central government and the nineteen largest cities in the Netherlands.

The Major Cities Memorandum has four main components: employment, education, health and welfare, and public safety. Initially, agreements or 'contracts' were drawn up between the government and the four largest conurbations: Amsterdam, Rotterdam, Utrecht and The Hague (subsequent agreements will be developed with fifteen additional cities). Each agreement runs for four years – from 1995 to 1998 – and contains obligations and objectives for both parties. The principal problems which the agreements will address are high unemployment, immigration and insecurity and the social and cultural divisions which these engender. Among the aims of the agreements are the reduction of crime and fear of crime.

Inter-Ministerial Group

The government has allocated approximately £100 million over a period of four years (and £40 million per year thereafter) to combat juvenile crime in all nineteen cities. An additional £8 million has been allocated for tackling drug-related anti-social behaviour. An Inter-

Ministerial Group (comprising the interior, justice, welfare, social affairs and education ministries) has been set up to develop a plan on the basis that responsibility should not rest solely with the justice ministry. To reflect this inter-departmental dimension, the initiative is called 'Youth and Safety' rather than adopting the narrower reference point of youth crime.

Nevertheless, developing a jointly agreed policy with recommendations for action has not been achieved without difficulties. Initially, some ministries (especially the education ministry) were reluctant to cooperate in the development of policy in an area for which they did not feel responsible. Improvements in cooperation (and consequent reductions in territoriality) were achieved over time. These improvements came about largely by demonstrating that:

- the causes of crime were predominantly located within the remits of other government departments (especially education)
- unbeknown to individual agencies, most young offenders and young people at risk of offending had multiple contacts with a variety of agencies
- solutions not only had to be local, but had to incorporate elements of justice and welfare
- the problems of cities were overwhelming; to have any realistic chance of tackling them, an integrated approach was essential.

The fact that this initiative came with considerable funds which other ministries were keen to exploit probably also played a considerable part in improving inter-departmental cooperation.

To ensure cooperation at the local level, meetings were set up between the Inter-Ministerial Group and all the local agencies concerned. Some agencies (especially public prosecution departments) needed a little persuasion and there were also difficulties with administrative boundaries.

Rotterdam: an example of a city agreement

Each agreement contains quantifiable targets and each city is obliged (but not compelled) to reach such targets. Taking the Rotterdam agreement as an example, the city undertakes to reduce the number of young people who get into trouble with the police by 30 per cent over a four year period. Other targets contained in the Rotterdam agreement include:

- guaranteeing at least 10 per cent of all young people on training schemes fully paid apprenticeships upon completion (this is known as the youth work guarantee scheme)
- increasing the number of training places and apprenticeships by 15 per cent per year
- improving training results by 10 per cent
- reducing the number of early school leavers by 35 per cent and increasing the pass rate of school pupils by 25 per cent over four years
- ensuring 90 per cent of school leavers get a job within a year of leaving school
- a 10 per cent increase in the use of community service orders and referrals to HALT projects (see below).

Public Safety Plans

To achieve targeted reductions in juvenile crime, each city is developing Public Safety Plans, involving the police, the local authority, private organisations and residents' associations. These plans comprise two main elements. Firstly, large numbers of supervisory staff are being employed in public spaces and on public transport. In effect, the Dutch are using people (predominantly the unemployed) rather than technology to carry out surveillance in public areas. Secondly, a range of preventive and repressive measures are being implemented to tackle juvenile crime.

Targeting those at risk of offending

The latter requires each city to prepare an action plan which outlines the tasks of each local agency and how those at risk of offending will be identified and targeted. Teachers, school doctors and health workers play a central role in the identification process. The key to success is considered to be early, fast and consequential intervention. A client following system is developed through which the police, the public prosecution and the youth welfare agency keep track of individual young offenders and those at risk of offending. Information is exchanged between these three agencies on regular basis, although there are still difficult problems of confidentiality and data protection to solve.

An integrated youth policy

In Rotterdam, efforts to combat juvenile crime are linked into an integrated youth strategy for all children and young people up to the age of 24. Over one third of young people in Rotterdam are from ethnic minorities and one of the aims of this strategy is to prevent situations developing, or continuing, which could give rise to emotional and behavioural problems. One aspect of the integrated youth policy is therefore the preventive policy, which comprises five elements:

- the continuous monitoring of children at crucial points in their development
- informing parents early about how to recognise and deal with their child's behavioural problems
- providing support to parents and schools
- providing more resources for clinics charged with fostering the social and emotional development and behaviour of children and young people
- developing alternative ways of regulating negative emotions and resolving behaviour problems.

Lessons for the UK?

There are interesting parallels and differences between the Netherlands and the UK. The Netherlands is one of the few countries to have developed a national strategy which includes negotiated contracts between central and local government to deliver specific prevention targets. In addition, 1 per cent of the criminal justice budget has been allocated for prevention (compared to 0.37 per cent in the UK) and the director of prevention is assigned the same status as the director of prisons in the justice department.

One of the measures which has attracted much interest in the UK is the Civic Guards scheme, already referred to in the earlier discussion about policing. It began in Dordrecht in 1989 and has been copied throughout the country. The aim is to restore order and a sense of safety to public spaces, especially town centres, following the withdrawal of police from these areas into more serious criminal work. This challenge was also seen as an opportunity to create jobs, especially for publicly committed, unemployed young people. In 1996, there was a Civic Guard presence in 120 towns and cities employing over 2,000 young people full time, though initially on short-term contracts. The funding of guards for 49 towns has now been agreed by central government and the long-term funding of the schemes seems assured. Surveys show increased satisfaction by the public with their town and city centres.[169]

Some authorities in the UK are showing a keen interest in the Civic Guards idea which they hope to fund through the Single Regeneration Budget. Since 1995, the town centre of Accrington in Lancashire has been patrolled from 8.00 am to 8.00 pm on a rota basis by a team of nine community safety wardens. As in the Netherlands, these young staff wear uniforms and carry radios directly linked to the police. Local response has been very positive.[170] Other UK towns and cities are employing 'city ambassadors'. The obvious parallel is with the popularity and rapid spread of CCTV in the town and city centres of the UK. A cost-benefit analysis of the two approaches would be interesting.

Summary

In this chapter, a framework for a national strategy has been proposed and responsibility assigned to both central government and local authorities working closely with the police and others. Focusing on high crime neighbourhoods and in town and city centres is the most promising way of making a significant difference to offence and offender rates. Building crime prevention into mainstream services is the most promising means of extending the scope of crime prevention and community safety beyond individual projects. The costs and benefits of prevention have been discussed and evidence submitted that crime prevention can be cost effective. Finally, the strategy developed in the Netherlands has been described and its implications for the UK noted. One conclusion that may be drawn from this chapter is that there is substantial scope for 'raising our game'. The potential for reducing crime problems is much greater than most people realise.

Conclusion

Faced with the choice between changing one's mind and proving there is no need to do so, almost everybody gets busy with the proof.
J K Galbraith

In its proposals for preventing crime, this book has emphasised preventive action rather than moral condemnation. This is not because it wishes to excuse criminal behaviour. Nor does it wish to deny that individual offenders are responsible for their crimes and should be held to account for them. The concept of individual responsibility – within a system in which government and citizens accept they have mutual rights and responsibilities – is fundamental to most people's idea of a good society.

Furthermore, society, through its government and other institutions, is right to assert certain values and standards. It should state unequivocally that crime is unacceptable. In particular, it is right to express its moral outrage against violent crimes such as racial harassment, domestic violence and crime against the elderly and children which violate the most basic human right of all – freedom from violence. In doing so, it helps create a climate which is less tolerant of such behaviour. These standards are backed up by the law. For the majority, this will be sufficient to ensure a reasonable level of compliance.

At the same time, exhortations against anti-social behaviour and crime, and calls for more moral behaviour by the young are unlikely, on their own, to make people inclined to criminality behave differently. Generations of politicians and religious leaders since the time of

Hammurabi have discovered this unwelcome fact. Nor does the apparatus of the criminal justice system and the threat of tougher sentences control criminal behaviour very successfully.

The decision to offend is not a purely rational choice based on a logical assessment of the costs and risks involved. It is also a product of a culture that has to be changed by something more interventionist than sentencing policy.

If we want to prevent *crime* in those areas where high standards do not prevail, we must intervene in the process which leads to a crime being committed. We must focus on the crime-prone situation and make the crime more difficult to commit. Similarly, if we want to reduce *criminality*, we must intervene in the circumstances that prevent some young people learning to behave socially, failing to respect others and growing up to believe that they have no stake in society. Some of the ultimate causes of criminality (for example, changes to the labour market) are difficult even for government to influence. There are others, as we have seen, about which we can do something.

The point is that we have to do something. We have to reduce risk factors that can lead to criminality and strengthen the protective factors that guard against it. We know how to do this although there is still much to be learned. Recognising the potential of this approach implies the need for a fundamental shift in the way we think about crime and its prevention. What is needed is a national prevention strategy. From central government, this will require clear leadership, incentives, guidance, priorities, objectives and some resources. It will involve investment in research and evaluation so that preventive practice can be tested and refined. It will involve scrutiny of draft legislation to ensure that it does not unintentionally increase crime, perhaps through 'crime impact statements'.[171]

Local authorities will be required to prepare annual, costed community safety plans. These should involve rigorous, data-led initiatives which are carefully planned, implemented and evaluated. The plans should aim to 'mainstream' prevention so that it becomes integral to local governance rather than characterised by short-term, individual *ad hoc* projects, as at present. There is scope for refocusing resources and obtaining much better preventive value from existing expenditure.

Comprehensive approaches in high crime neighbourhoods should involve a thematic approach that: i) makes crime more difficult, less rewarding and more risky to commit (safer neighbourhoods); ii) takes steps to reduce offending among teenagers and young adults (opportunities for young people); and iii) develops preventive services for families and children to reduce the risk factors associated with anti-social behaviour and later offending (early childhood prevention). While the problems of such areas will not be resolved by prevention strategies alone, there is plenty of evidence that well-planned preventive measures can make a difference – sometimes a big difference. They can reduce the impact of crime on victims, improve the life chances of young people by halting their drift into offending and enhance the quality of life for everyone.

Of particular importance is the need to improve the way young men are brought up. Men are responsible for most crime and for the most serious crime. Improving the parenting, schooling and subsequent opportunities for young men from disadvantaged areas is one of the biggest challenges in social policy.

The approach described in this book is affordable, particularly if attention is given to obtaining added preventive value from existing resources and implementing measures which are cost effective. It is implementable, providing clear achievable plans are drawn up and someone is assigned responsibility for implementing them. It is practical – many of the measures proposed in this book are drawn from tried and tested practice. It is popular – the public want to see more done to prevent crime and enhance safety. With regard to offenders, they also believe that more should be done to 'catch them earlier'. As we have seen, the approach makes economic sense.

Prevention is not being presented as a complete answer to crime. That would be hopelessly utopian. It is being promoted as an important – and undervalued – element of a crime control strategy that can reduce crime, criminality and fear, thus freeing up the criminal justice agencies from the excessive demands that prevent them from tackling serious crime, providing justice promptly and rehabilitating offenders.

To bring about this shift in policy will require the vision to see what can be achieved and political leadership of a high order to bring it about. But it will be worth it. There will be many benefits which will be felt well beyond the criminal justice sector. The challenge now is to invest in prevention before problems become too big to prevent.

Appendix one: note on crime statistics

From Mayhew P, Aye Maung N and Mirrlees-Black C, 1993, The 1992 British crime survey, *Home Office Research Study 132, HMSO, London.*

The statistics of recorded crime do not necessarily portray the full picture of crime experienced by society at large. Estimates derived from the *British crime survey* (BCS) suggest that of all offences committed only about half are reported to the police and fewer than one third recorded. For a variety of reasons, many offences are not reported to the police and, of those that are reported, some go unrecorded and this picture varies considerably between different offences.

All crime surveys have shown that a great many crimes go unreported to the police, mainly because they are not seen as sufficiently serious, or because calling the police is not thought to provide any remedy. But few have tried, as the BCS does, to relate the number of reported offences to the number recorded by the police in order to estimate the extent of unrecorded crime. Offences which are not reported or recorded make up the so-called 'dark figure' of crime and the BCS has been able to show the size of this for different offences.

The count of crime in the BCS differs from that of the police as follows:

- The survey includes unreported as well as reported offences. The largest discrepancy will be in the two sets of figures for poorly unreported crimes such as vandalism. The BCS count of unreported crime however is not simply a count of incidents 'not worthy worrying about', a good number of unreported incidents are judged to be serious.
- It also includes some categories of crime – such as common assaults – which are excluded from the 'notifiable offences' series collated by the police. (Other offences are covered by both series, but cannot always be matched. Household thefts are an example, being subsumed in police statistics in the very broad category of 'other thefts'.)
- It excludes crimes against organisations (for example, fraud, shoplifting, fare evasion, commercial burglary and robbery).

- It excludes so-called 'victimless' crimes (such as drug and alcohol misuse), consensual sexual offences, or crimes where people may not be aware of having been victimised, as in an assortment of frauds.

Author's note

Generally, all crime statistics should be prefaced with a health warning. There are a wide range of changing factors that may influence the willingness of the public to report crimes to the police or to researchers. This especially applies to the willingness of women and children to report crimes of abuse by family or household members. International comparisons can be even more problematic. These qualifications should be borne in mind when considering the data presented in the following tables.

Appendix two: selected crime statistics tables

From Barclay GC, ed, 1996, Information on the criminal justice system in England and Wales, *Digest 3, Home Office Research and Statistics Department, London.*

Table 1. Crimes recorded by the police, 1876 to 1996

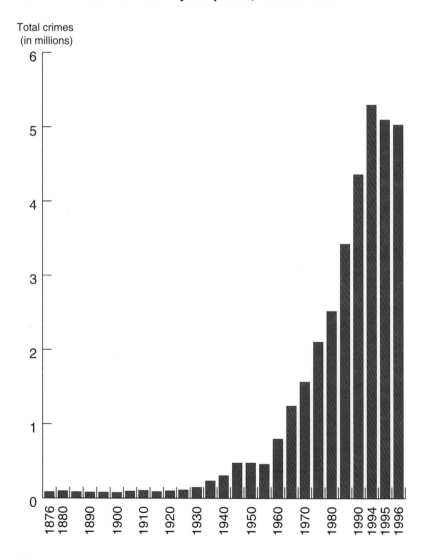

Total crimes (in millions)

Table 2. Levels of recorded and unrecorded crime, 1993

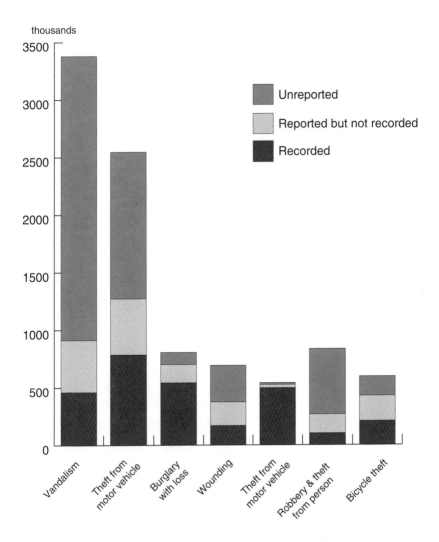

thousands

Legend:
- Unreported
- Reported but not recorded
- Recorded

Categories (x-axis):
Vandalism, Theft from motor vehicle, Burglary with loss, Wounding, Theft from motor vehicle, Robbery & theft from person, Bicycle theft

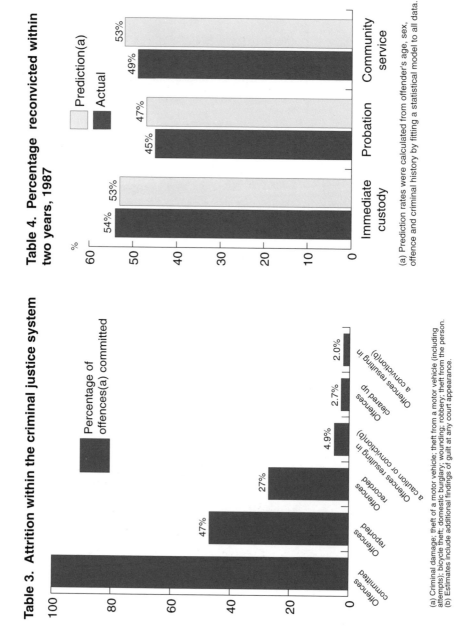

Table 3. Attrition within the criminal justice system

Percentage of offences(a) committed

- Offences committed: 100
- Offences reported: 47%
- Offences recorded: 27%
- Offences resulting in a caution or conviction(b): 4.9%
- Offences cleared up: 2.7%
- Offences resulting in a conviction(b): 2.0%

(a) Criminal damage; theft of a motor vehicle (including attempts); bicycle theft; domestic burglary; wounding; robbery; theft from the person.
(b) Estimates include additional findings of guilt at any court appearance.

Table 4. Percentage reconvicted within two years, 1987

Prediction(a)
Actual

- Immediate custody: Actual 54%, Prediction(a) 53%
- Probation: Actual 45%, Prediction(a) 47%
- Community service: Actual 49%, Prediction(a) 53%

(a) Prediction rates were calculated from offender's age, sex, offence and criminal history by fitting a statistical model to all data.

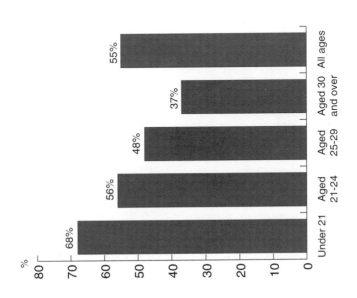

Table 5. Reconviction rate by age

Under 21	Aged 21-24	Aged 25-29	Aged 30 and over	All ages
68%	56%	48%	37%	55%

Table 6. Reconviction rate by gender

Males	Females
56%	40%

Notes

1. Home Office Research and Statistics Department, 1995, *Information on the criminal justice system in England and Wales*, HMSO, London, 1.

2. See note 1.

3. See note 1, 67-68

4. See note 1, 25.

5. See note 1, 19.

6. See note 1, 57.

7. Graham J and Bowling B, 1995, *Young people and crime*, Home Office Research Study 145, HMSO, London.

8. see note 7.

9. Crime Concern /Thames Valley Partnership, 1994, *Counting the cost*, Crime Concern, Swindon, 1-2.

10. See, for example: Mori /Barnados, 1995, *The facts of life: the changing face of childhood*, Barnardos, London.

11. See for example: Lea J and Young J, 1984, *What is to be done about law and order?*, Penguin, London; Mayhew P, Aye Maung N and Mirrlees-Black C, 1993, *The 1992 British crime survey*, Home Office Research Study No 132, HMSO, London; Hope T, 1996, 'Community, crime and inequality in England and Wales' in Bennett T, ed, 1996, *Preventing crime and disorder*, Cropwood Series, University of Cambridge, Cambridge.

12. See note 11 (Mayhew *et al*).

13. Unpublished police data acquired for Small Business and Crime Initiative, Leicester, Crime Concern, Swindon, 1996.

14. Husain S, 1995, *Cutting crime in rural areas*, Crime Concern, Swindon.

15. Smith L, 1989, *Domestic violence: an overview of the literature*, Home Office Research Study No 107, HMSO, London.

16. Department of Education and Science /Welsh Office, 1988, *Discipline in schools,* report of the Committee of Enquiry chaired by Lord Elton, HMSO, London.

17. Hough M, 1995, *Anxiety about crime: findings from the 1994 British crime survey*, Home Office Research Study No 147, HMSO, London; Mayhew P, 1994, *Findings from the international crime survey*, Research Findings No 8, Home Office, London.

18. Smith D, 1995, speech to Crime Concern conference, Edinburgh, unpublished.

19. For example: Gallup's *Political and economic index* (September 1993) found that 82 per cent of those questioned were 'not very' or 'not at all' confident that the Government will succeed in reducing crime substantially. Another indicator of an absence of public confidence can be found on page seven of the Home Affairs Select Committee Report on Juvenile Offenders in July 1993 (Home Affairs Select Committee, Session 1992-93, HC 441-I, *Juvenile Offenders Memoranda of Evidence*, HMSO, London). The committee explained that it had 'decided on an enquiry both because of public concern about the level of juvenile crime and because of the apparent inability of the criminal justice system to deal effectively with it'.

20. Home Office, 1994, *Criminal statistics England and Wales*, HMSO, London, 15, 125.

21. Farrington DP, 1996, *Understanding and preventing youth crime*, Joseph Rowntree Foundation, York, 2.

22. Audit Commission, 1996, *Misspent youth: young people and crime*, Audit Commission, London.

23. See note 20, 134, 139.

24. NACRO, 1993, *Community provision for young people in the youth justice system*, NACRO, London and 'News from Northumbria Police', press release, 11 January 1996, Northumbria Police.

25. See note 20, 165-166.

26. *Hansard*, 23 January 1996.

27. See note 19 (Home Affairs Select Committee) para 89 and note 24 (NACRO, 1993).

28. Research indicates that the programmes which reduce re-offending by persistent offenders most effectively:

• are based on behaviour and skills training

• help individuals into employment or back to school

• involve interventions of six months or more, with at least two contacts per week and/or more than 100 total contact hours

• are community-based, because it is easier to relate lessons learned to real life

• have consistent aims and methods

• are delivered by well trained and skilled practitioners

• are carefully matched to the offender's needs.

Research also shows that approaches which tend to be ineffective with persistent offenders are:

• general counselling, casework, family counselling and psycho-dynamic therapy – which may increase self-esteem but do not reduce anti-social behaviour

• unstructured groups – potentially fostering communications which reinforce offending behaviour and

• exclusively punishment-based programmes – which tend to harden attitudes, without causing offenders to reflect on their behaviour.
See note 22.

29. See note 17 (Hough, 1995) and note 20.

30. *The Independent*, 19 July 1996.

31. Royal College of Psychiatrists, 1996, 'Royal College criticises community care policy', press release, July 1996, Royal College of Psychiatrists, London.

32. Although the main focus of this book is residential neighbourhoods, it is worth noting that safety and crime reduction in town and city centres and on public transport networks has received a good deal of attention from the Association of Town and City Centre Managers, the Home Office, the Departments of the Environment and Transport and many local authorities. The most effective strategies derive from a careful analysis of crime problems and involve a variety of responses such as improved design and lighting, safer pedestrian corridors, safe car parks, work with the managers of licensed premises, deployment of community wardens, diversification of amenities and so on.

Government funding has enabled many towns and cities to install CCTV systems which have often led to impressive reductions in crime. They are most likely to have a long-term impact if they are installed as part of a package of measures tailored to particular centres rather than regarded as an all-purpose crime prevention tool.

See also the discussion of the Dutch Civic Guards scheme at the end of chapter five and the views of Ken Worpole and Liz Greenhalgh (Worpole K and Greenhalgh L, 1996, *The freedom of the city*, Demos, London) where they argue that crime prevention in public spaces will be better achieved by generating more use of these areas and ensuring that they are supervised by patrolling staff as well as by CCTV.

33. Bottoms AE and Wiles P, 1996, 'Understanding crime prevention in late modern societies' in Bennett, 1996 (see note 11), 28.

34. Pyle DJ, 1995, *Cutting the costs of crime*, Hobard Paper 129, Institute for Economic Affairs, London, 14, 27-29.

35. Martinson R, 1974 'What works? Questions and answers about prison reform' in *The Public Interest*, no 35, 22-54; and 'Martinson attacks his own earlier work' in *Criminal Justice Newsletter*, 9 December 1978.

36. See for example note 19 (Gallup, 1993). When asked what would do most to prevent crime, there was strong support for preventive measures.

37. Etzioni A, 1993, *The spirit of community*, Simon and Schuster, New York.

38. Graham J, 1990, *Crime prevention strategies in Europe and North America*, conference report, Helsinki Institute for Crime Prevention, Helsinki, 6-7.

39. Steinmetz C, 1990 cited in Graham, 1990 (see note 38), 6.

40. Clarke R and Hough J, 1984, *Crime and police effectiveness*, Home Office Study No 79, HMSO, London; see also note 34.

41. See note 38, 7.

42. Shapland J, Hibbert J, L'Anson J, Sorsby A and Wild R, 1995, *Milton Keynes criminal justice audit*, Institute of the Study of the Legal Profession, University of Sheffield, Sheffield.

43. Curtis L, 1990, *Youth investment and community reconstruction: street lessons on*

drugs and crime for the nineties, Eisenhower Foundation, Washington DC, 8-9.

44. Currie E, 1985, *Confronting crime: an American challenge*, Pantheon, New York.

45. *Criminal Justice Newsletter*, vol 21 no 18.

46. Investigative articles on the criminal justice system in *Los Angeles Times*, 17-22 December 1990.

47. Eisenhower Foundation, 1989, *The national drug control strategy and inner city policy*, testimony before the Select Committee on Narcotics Abuse and Control, US House of Representatives, Washington DC.

48. Smith DJ, 1983, *Police and policing in London*, Policy Studies Institute, London.

49. Audit Commission, 1996, *Streetwise: effective police patrol*, Audit Commission, London, 48-49.

50. See note 49.

51. Skogan WG, 1990, *Disorder and decline: crime and the spiral of decay in American neighbourhoods*, New York Free Press, New York.

52. Hope T, 1988, 'Support for Neighbourhood Watch: a British crime survey analysis' in Hope T and Shaw M, eds, *Communities and crime reduction*, Home Office Research and Planning Unit, London.

53. See, for example, note 21, 28; Schorr L, 1988, *Within our reach: breaking down the cycle of disadvantage*, Doubleday, New York; Howell JC, Krisberg B, Hawkins JP and Wilson JJ, 1995, *A source book, serious, violent, chronic juvenile offenders*, Sage Publications, London; and Nicholson L, 1995, *What works in situational crime prevention? A literature review*, The Scottish Office

Central Research Unit, Edinburgh.

54. For a summary see: note 21; Hawkins JD, Catalano RF and associates, 1992, *Communities that care: action for drug abuse prevention*, Jossey-Bass, San Francisco; and Utting D, Bright J and Henrickson C, 1993, *Crime and the family: improving childrearing and reducing delinquency*, Family Policy Studies Centre, London.

55. See note 54 (Hawkins *et al*, 1992).

56. Emler N and Reicher S, 1995, *Adolescence and delinquency*, Blackwell, Oxford.

57. See note 7.

58. See note 54 (Utting *et al*, 1993).

59. The most developed initiative of this kind is the Communities that Care (CTC) process devised by Professor David Hawkins and colleagues at the University of Washington in Seattle (see note 54 (Hawkins *et al*, 1992)). CTC has been adopted as a major element of the federal government's Comprehensive Strategy for Serious, Violent and Chronic Juvenile Offenders (see Office for Juvenile Justice and Delinquency Prevention, 1995, *Guide for implementing a comprehensive strategy for serious violence and chronic juvenile offenders*, US Department of Justice, Washington DC). This approach is being developed in the UK by the Joseph Rowntree Foundation. It also underpins the approach to criminality prevention promoted by Crime Concern (see Crime Concern, 1995, *Criminality prevention: a briefing paper*, Crime Concern, Swindon). Generally, much more attention needs to be paid to evaluating 'promising approaches' in the UK so that we have a much better understanding of what works under what circumstances.

60. Although the focus is the neighbourhood, it is likely that the benefits of successful programmes may be felt more widely – in town and city centres, in lower crime neighbourhoods, on public transport networks and in public spaces generally.

61. See note 53 (Schorr, 1988); note 21; note 54 (Hawkins *et al*, 1992).

62. See note 54 (Utting *et al*, 1993).

63. Ontario Ministry for Community and Social Services, 1988, *Better beginnings, better futures*, Ontario Ministry for Community and Social Services, Ontario, Canada.

64. See note 53 (Schorr, 1988).

65. See note 53 (Schorr, 1988), 156-163; note 63.

66. Van der Eyken W, 1982, *Homestart: a four year evaluation*, Homestart UK, Leicester (revised 1990).

67. Halpearn and Weiss, 1990, *Helping families to grow strong: new directions in public policy*, Harvard Family Research Project, Harvard University, Harvard, Massachusetts; Halpearn and Weiss, 1988, *What is known about the effectiveness of family orientated early childhood programmes,* manuscript, Harvard Family Research Project, Harvard University, Harvard, Massachusetts; Lally R, Manigone P and Honig A, 1988, 'Long range impact of early intervention with low income children and their families' in Powell D, ed, *Parent education as early childhood intervention*, Ablex, Norwood, NJ.

68. Davis H, 1996, *An independent evaluation of Parent Link*, Parent Network, London.

69. Smith C and Pugh G, 1996, *Learning to be a parent*, Joseph Rowntree Foundation, York.

70. See note 49.

71. Smith C, 1996, *Developing parenting programmes*, National Children's Bureau, London, 33.

72. See note 71.

73. Berrueta-Clement JR, Schweinhart LJ, Barnett WS, Epstein AS and Weikart DP, 1984, *Changed lives: the effects of the Perry pre-school program on youths through age nineteen*, High/Scope Foundation, Ypsilanti, Michigan.

74. Schweinhart LJ, Barnes HV and Weikart DP, 1993, *Significant benefits: the High/Scope Perry pre-school study through age 27*, High/Scope Foundation, Ypsilanti, Michigan.

75. High/Scope Education Foundation, 1990, *Factsheets*, High/Scope Education Foundation, Ypsilanti, Michigan.

76. Note that the results of this study were supported by other research studies, one of which involved a meta-analysis of eleven American pre-school programmes: Lazar I, Darington R, Murray H, Royce J and Snipper A, 1982, *Lasting effects of early education*, Monographs of the Society for Research in Child Development 47, Society for Research in Child Development, London, 1-151.

77. There is some evidence for this. The study on which this conclusion is based compared three approaches: High/Scope, a more conventional nursery school and a 'direct instruction' class. The High/Scope and nursery school approaches both emphasised child-initiated activities in which young children pursued their own interests with staff support and guidance. The direct instruction approach, by contrast, focused on academic skills and expected young children respond to questions with the right answers. The study found that all three approaches improved young children's intellectual performance considerably, with the average IQs of all three groups rising by 27 points in a year. But by the age of fifteen, the two groups whose curricula had emphasised child-initiated activities report only half as much delinquent activity as the direct instruction group. Schweinhart L, Weikart C and Lerner M, 1986, 'Consequences of three pre-school curriculum models through age fifteen' in *Early Childhood Research Quarterly*, vol 1, 15-45.

78. Hayes R and Saunders L, 1992, *Social policy issues research report*, manuscript, Kent County Council, Maidstone.

79. Sylva K and Moss P, 1992, *Learning before school*, Briefing No 8, National Commission on Education, London.

80. Osborn AF and Millbank JE, 1987, *The effects of early education*, Clarendon, Oxford, 206.

81. See note 80, 238-239.

82. See for example: note 80, 240; New L and David M, 1985, *For the children's sake*, Penguin, London; Strathclyde Regional Council, 1985, *Under fives final report of the member/officer group*, Glasgow Council, Glasgow; Jowett S and Sylva K, 1986, 'Does kind of pre-school matter?' in *Educational Research*, vol 1, 21-31; and Finch J, 1984, 'A first class environment? Working class playgroups as pre-school experience' in *British Education Research Journal*, vol 10 no 1, 3-17.

83. Sylva K, 1988, 'Does early intervention work?' in *Archives of Disease in Childhood*, vol 64, 1103-1104.

84. See note 54.

85. Audit Commission, 1994, *Seen but*

not heard: coordinating community child health and social services for children in need, HMSO, London.

86. Rutter M, 1972, 'Maternal deprivation realised' in Rutter M and Madge N, 1976, *Cycles of disadvantage: a review of research*, Heinmann Educational Books, London, 132.

87. Clarke, 1968, 'Learning and human development' in *British Journal of Psychology*, vol 114, 1061-1077, cited in Rutter and Madge, 1976 (see note 86).

88. For a summary, see note 21; note 38; and Graham J and Bennett T, 1995, *Crime prevention strategies in Europe and North America*, European Institute for Crime Prevention and Control, Helsinki.

89. See for example: Rutter M *et al*, 1979, *Fifteen thousand hours: secondary schools and their effect on children*, Open Books, London; Mortimore P *et al*, 1988, *School matters: junior years*, Open Books, Wells; and Smith DJ and Tomlinson S, 1989, *School effect: a study of multi-racial comprehensives*, Policy Studies Institute, London.

90. National Commission on Education, 1996, *Success against the odds*, Routledge, London.

91. See note 38.

92. There are limits, of course, to what individual schools can do. The most well known study in this area also found an association between 'academic balance' and delinquency (See note 89 (Rutter *et al*, 1979)). As might be expected, delinquency rates and non-attendance were lower in schools which had a relatively high concentration of pupils in the upper ability bands at intake and higher in those with a high proportion of low ability pupils although there were no

significant differences in behaviour in school. It seems that schools with a high proportion of less able pupils can influence pupil behaviour in school by good management more than they can delinquency outside of school. This ability balance is a matter over which schools and Local Education Authorities have diminishing control. See note 89 (Smith and Tomlinson, 1989), 301.

93. See note 59 (Office for Juvenile Justice and Delinquency, 1995), 127-128

94. *Missing out. Truancy: the consequences and the solutions*, 1991, TVAM.

95. Gray J and Jefferson D, 1990, *Truancy in secondary schools among fifth year pupils*, Education Research Centre, Sheffield University, Sheffield.

96. See note 7.

97. See note 38.

98. Department of Education and Science, 1989, *Attendance at School*, Education Observed Series No 13, HMSO, London, 28

99. Cities in schools, *Action for truants*, Cities in Schools, London.

100. NERS data on exclusions: 1991/92 – 3,833; 1992/93 – 11,181; 1994/95 – 11,084

101. See note 7, 42.

102. See note 98, 28.

103. *The Observer*, 9 February 1992.

104. See for example, the partnership between Solihull Metropolitan Borough Council and Crime Concern's Cascade peer-led drug education project.

105. Department for Education, 1994, *Bullying: don't suffer in silence. An anti-bullying pack for schools*, HMSO, London.

106. Mortimore P, 1991, 'School effectiveness research: which way at the cross roads?' in *School Effectiveness and School Improvement*, vol 2 no 3, 223.

107. Mortimore P, 1991, 'Bucking the trends: promoting successful urban education', *Times Education Supplement*/Greenwich Annual Lecture.

108. Riley D and Shaw M, 1985, *Parental supervision and juvenile delinquency*, Home Office Research Study No 83, HMSO, London.

109. See note 88 (Graham and Bennett, 1995), 32-41.

110. Graham J and Smith DI, 1992, *Diversion from offending: the role of the Youth Service*, Crime Concern, Swindon.

111. See note 110; see also France A and Wiles P, 1996, *The Youth Action Scheme. A report of the national evaluation*, Department for Education and Employment, London.

112. Taken from: Osborne S and Shaftoe H, 1995, *Safer neighbourhoods? Successes and failures in crime prevention*, Safer Neighbourhoods Unit, London.

113. Webb J, 1994, *The Runcorn Youth Action Project*, manuscript, Crime Concern, Swindon.

114. Webb J, 1996, *The Dalston Youth Project: an evaluation of Programme 1*, manuscript, Crime Concern, Swindon.

115. See note 7.

116. Cited in a report of the Conference on Employment Training and Offenders, 16 March 1988, Association of Chief Officers of Probation, The Apex Trust and NACRO, London.

117. Wilkinson C, 1995, *The drop out society: young people on the margin*, Youth Work Press, Leicester.

118. Newcastle is one city which has experience of developing economic development work with young people. Key principles are:

- real partnership approach between agencies
- a range of initiatives such basic skills training, community or college training, and economic development work with young people
- the importance of a broader, area-based employment strategy
- use of detached youth work to encourage participation
- clear goals and outcomes
- a realistic acceptance of what can be achieved.

A key requirement is an area-based employment development worker to coordinate work at a neighbourhood level. Evidence given by Newcastle City Council to a Crime Concern Task Group, May 1994.

119. Employment Policy Institute, 1996, 'Unemployment: A modest proposal', vol, 10 no 6.

120. Rees G, Instance D and Williamson H, 1994, *Young people not in education, training or employment in South Glamorgan*, South Glamorgan Training and Enterprise Council, Cardiff; and note 59 (Crime Concern, 1995).

121. See note 44.

122. See note 7.

123. Association of Chief Officers of Probation, 1993, *Social circumstances of young offenders under supervision*, Association of Chief Officers of Probation, London.

124. Centrepoint, 1992, *Homeless and hungry*, Centrepoint, London.

125. Evans A, 1996, *We didn't choose to be homeless*, CHAR, London.

126. See note 124.

127. See note 7.

128. National Board for Crime Prevention, 1994, *Wise after the event: tackling repeat victimisation*, Home

Office, London.

129. Webb J, 1996, *Direct line homesafe: an evaluation of the first year*, manuscript, Crime Concern, Swindon.

130. Department of the Environment, 1991, *A handbook of estate improvement: part 2, external areas*, HMSO, London.

131. Coleman A, 1987, *Utopia on trial*, Hilary Rose, London.

132. Wilson S, 1978, 'Vandalism and defensible space on London housing estates' in Clarke RUG and Mayhew P, eds, 1980, *Designing out crime*, HMSO, London.

133. See note 51.

134. Page D, 1996, 'Still swimming against the tide?' in *London Housing News*, summer 1996.

135. Power A, 1987, *The PEP guide to local housing estate management*, Department of the Environment, London.

136. Hope T and Foster J, 1991, *Conflicting forces: changing the dynamics of crime and community on a problem estate*, paper given at British Criminology Conference, 25 July 1991, York.

137. Hope T and Foster J, 1993, *Housing, community and crime: the impact of the Priority Estates Project*, Home Office Research Study No 131, HMSO, London.

138. On Swansea's Townhill North Estate in 1994-95, there was a reduction in the number of empty flats from 47 to 27, resulting in savings of £72,280 in rent loss and security screening; a reduction in vandalism (loss of heating systems and damage caused) by 80 per cent saving £104,000; a reduction in theft from cars by 50 per cent; and a reduction of calls to the police relating to nuisance of 75 per cent. Wardens prevented seventeen genuine attempts of burglary and the estate fell from first to fourth place in the City's crime league. City and County of Swansea Department of Housing memorandum, 25 October 1996.

139. Power A, 1995, *Swimming against the tide*, Joseph Rowntree Foundation, York.

140. Leigh A, Read T and Tilley N, 1996, *Problem solving orientated policing Britpop*, Home Office Police Research Group Paper 75, HMSO, London.

141. NACRO, 1996, *Crime, community and change: taking action against the Kingsmead Estate in Hackney*, NACRO, London.

142. See note 49.

143. Department of the Environment, 1993, *Crime prevention on housing estates*, HMSO, London, 94-97.

144. See note 140.

145. Information from Sampson A and Phillip C, 1996, *Taking action against perpetrators of racial harassment* (forthcoming) presented at Home Office seminar, *Preventing repeat victimisation*, 22 April 1996, Home Office, London.

146. See note 145.

147. See note 141.

148. NACRO, 1992, *Youth activity unit's annual review*, NACRO, London.

149. Home Office, 1984, *Crime prevention*, interdepartmental circular 8/84, Home Office, London.

150. Home Office, 1993, *A practical guide to crime prevention for local partnerships*, HMSO, London, 5.

151. Crime Concern, 1996, *Reducing crime and criminality in high crime neighbourhoods*, Briefing Paper No 3, Crime Concern, Swindon.

152. Tilley N, 1993, *Understanding car parks, crime and CCTV: evaluation lessons* *for safer cities*, Home Office Police Research Group No 42, Home Office, London.

153. Welsh WN, Harris PW and Jenkins PH, 1996, 'Reducing over-representation of minorities in juvenile justice: development of community-based programmes in Pennsylvania' in *Crime and Delinquency*, vol 42 no 1, 76-78.

154. See note 150.

155. Reiner R, 1985, 'The politics of the police' in Hope T and Shaw M, eds, 1988, *Community and crime reduction*, HMSO, London.

156. See note 149.

157. Home Office, 1991, *Safer communities: the local delivery of crime prevention through the partnership approach*, Home Office, London.

158. Police Foundation/Policy Studies Institute, 1996, *The role and responsibilities of the police*, report of an independent inquiry, Police Foundation/ Policy Studies Institute, London.

159. *Municipal Journal*, 8 May 1996, no10.

160. Department of Health, 1996, *Children in need: report of an SSI national inspection of SSD Family Support Services 1993/95*, HMSO, London.

161. See note 85.

162. See note 143, 115-143.

163. Greenwood P, Model K, Rydell C and Chiesa J, 1996, *Diverting children from a life of crime. Measuring costs and benefits*, Rand Corporation, California.

164. Coopers & Lybrand/Prince's Trust, 1994, *Preventative strategy for young people in trouble*, Prince's Trust, London.

165. See note 29; and Home Office Crime Prevention Unit, Papers 13, 23 and 47, Home Office, London.

166. Tarling R, 1993, *Analysing offending*, Home Office, London.

167. See note 34.

168. Penal Affairs Consortium, 1994, *The case against the secure training order*, Penal Affairs Consortium, London.

169. Taylor I, 1996, 'Someone to watch over you' in *Return of the local*, *Demos Quarterly*, issue 9, 43.

170. See note 169.

171. Legislation which may have unintentionally led to an increase in crime includes the 1993 Education Act (which led to a threefold increase in school exclusions), the introduction of Compulsory Competitive Tendering in the 1993 Housing Act (which appears to be leading to a reduction in 'preventive management' by social landlords) and the regular imposition of tough budgetary constraints on local authorities (which has led to the virtual abolition of the youth service in some areas). No judgment is being made about the nature of this legislation. The point is that its impact on crime does not seem to have been considered or anticipated.

This is not only a matter for central government. It applies to decision making at a local level. In one county with a serious level of heroin addiction, general practitioners decided to stop prescribing Methadone in the same week as a Home Office report showed how Methadone prescription could significantly reduce drug related crime. While the introduction of competition among the providers of health and public services may bring benefits, it has also resulted in an unwillingness by some agencies to address problems which do not fall into their more restricted brief.